Narratives of Adult English Learners and Teachers

NEW PERSPECTIVES ON LANGUAGE AND EDUCATION

Founding Editor: Viv Edwards, *University of Reading, UK*

Series Editors: Phan Le Ha, *University of Hawaii at Manoa, USA* and Joel Windle, *Monash University, Australia.*

Two decades of research and development in language and literacy education have yielded a broad, multidisciplinary focus. Yet education systems face constant economic and technological change, with attendant issues of identity and power, community and culture. This series will feature critical and interpretive, disciplinary and multidisciplinary perspectives on teaching and learning, language and literacy in new times.

All books in this series are externally peer-reviewed.

Full details of all the books in this series and of all our other publications can be found on http://www.multilingual-matters.com, or by writing to Multilingual Matters, St Nicholas House, 31–34 High Street, Bristol BS1 2AW, UK.

NEW PERSPECTIVES ON LANGUAGE AND EDUCATION: 67
Ideas and Reflections in Practice

Narratives of Adult English Learners and Teachers

Practical Applications

Clarena Larrotta

MULTILINGUAL MATTERS
Bristol • Blue Ridge Summit

DOI https://doi.org/10.21832/LARROT3170
Library of Congress Cataloging in Publication Data
A catalog record for this book is available from the Library of Congress.
Names: Larrotta, Clarena – author.
Title: Narratives of Adult English learners and Teachers: Practical Applications/ Clarena Larrotta.
Description: Blue Ridge Summit, PA : Multilingual Matters, [2019] | Series: New Perspectives on Language and Education: 67 | Includes bibliographical references and index.
Identifiers: LCCN 2018052787| ISBN 9781788923170 (hbk : alk. paper) | ISBN 9781788923163 (pbk : alk. paper) | ISBN 9781788923200 (kindle)
Subjects: LCSH: English language—Study and teaching—Foreign speakers. | Adult students.
Classification: LCC PE1128.A2 L346 2019 | DDC 428.0071/5—dc23 LC record available at https://lccn.loc.gov/2018052787

British Library Cataloguing in Publication Data
A catalogue entry for this book is available from the British Library.

ISBN-13: 978-1-78892-317-0 (hbk)
ISBN-13: 978-1-78892-316-3 (pbk)

Multilingual Matters
UK: St Nicholas House, 31–34 High Street, Bristol BS1 2AW, UK.
USA: NBN, Blue Ridge Summit, PA, USA.

Website: www.multilingual-matters.com
Twitter: Multi_Ling_Mat
Facebook: https://www.facebook.com/multilingualmatters
Blog: www.channelviewpublications.wordpress.com

Copyright © 2019 Clarena Larrotta.

All rights reserved. No part of this work may be reproduced in any form or by any means without permission in writing from the publisher.

The policy of Multilingual Matters/Channel View Publications is to use papers that are natural, renewable and recyclable products, made from wood grown in sustainable forests. In the manufacturing process of our books, and to further support our policy, preference is given to printers that have FSC and PEFC Chain of Custody certification. The FSC and/or PEFC logos will appear on those books where full certification has been granted to the printer concerned.

Typeset by Nova Techset Private Limited, Bengaluru and Chennai, India.
Printed and bound in the UK by the CPI Books Group Ltd.
Printed and bound in the US by Thomson-Shore, Inc.

Contents

	Figures and Tables	viii
	Acknowledgments	ix
1	Introduction and Supporting Theories	1
	Narratives of ESL Learners and Teachers	1
	Book Content	2
	Conceptual Framework	3
	Case Study Method	7
	Narrative	8
	Conclusion	12
	Recommendations for Practice	12
	Discussion Questions (Group Activity)	12

Part 1: Learners' Voices

2	Learning to Enjoy Reading in ESL	15
	Community-based Programs	15
	Setting ESL Learning Goals for the Term	16
	Reading is Boring	17
	Reading for Pleasure	20
	Connecting Students' Lives with Classroom Work	21
	Alberto Fails the Test	22
	Conclusion	23
	Recommendations for Practice	23
	Discussion Questions (Group Activity)	24
3	ESL Adults Transitioning from Oral Language to Print	25
	Dialogue and Storytelling	25
	Teaching the Teacher: Doña Inés Blossoms	26
	Moving from Oral Language to Print	29
	Supporting Adults with Low Literacy Skills	32
	Conclusion	33
	Recommendations for Practice	33
	Discussion Questions (Group Activity)	34

4	Adults Building Confidence Through Family Literacy	35
	Intergenerational Reading	35
	The Reading Project	36
	Building Confidence	37
	Conclusion	43
	Recommendations for Practice	44
	Discussion Questions (Group Activity)	44
5	Adult ESL Learners' Motivations	45
	Motivation to Learn a Second Language	45
	The Adult ESL Learners	48
	Case Study 1: Learners Attending the English Conversation Club	48
	Case Study 2: Learners Attending an Evening ESL Class	53
	Conclusion	59
	Recommendations for Practice	60
	Discussion Questions (Group Activity)	61

Part 2: Teachers' Voices

6	ESL Instruction Through Religious Organizations	65
	Religious Organizations Serving Immigrants	65
	Conclusion	74
	Recommendations for Practice	74
	Discussion Questions (Group Activity)	75
7	Public Libraries Building Literate Communities	76
	Public Libraries Building Literate Communities	76
	Daisy's Experiences as Librarian and Coordinator	76
	Conclusion	84
	Recommendations for Practice	84
	Discussion Questions (Group Activity)	84
8	Engaged Scholarship Training TESOL Instructors	85
	Training TESOL Instructors	85
	Engaged Scholarship	86
	Conclusion	96
	Recommendations for Practice	97
	Discussion Questions (Group Activity)	97
9	Negotiating Adult ESL Curriculum	98
	Negotiating the Curriculum	98
	Becoming an Adult ESL Teacher	99
	Services Offered to Adult Learners	101
	Enrollment and Completion Issues	102
	When All in Class are Female	104
	Conclusion	109

Recommendations for Practice	109
Discussion Questions (Group Activity)	110
10 Conclusion	111
Learners' and Teachers' Voices	111
Emergent Themes Discussed in the Book Chapters	113
Theoretical Connections	118
Future Research	120
Concluding Thoughts	121
Appendix	122
Definition of Relevant Terms	122
References	124
Index	130

Figures and Tables

Figures

Figure 2.1 Photo of a Mexican coin provided by Alberto — 18
Figure 3.1 Image of agave plantation provided by Doña Inés — 28
Figure 4.1 Maria and her children working together — 36
Figure 5.1 Viviana — 49
Figure 5.2 Esperanza — 50
Figure 5.3 Mariela — 52
Figure 5.4 Raul — 54
Figure 5.5 Mauricio — 55
Figure 6.1 Community garden image provided by Sarah — 72
Figure 6.2 Refugee arrivals to the USA, 2016 — 73
Figure 7.1 Mondopads for the library — 81
Figure 8.1 Learner in a tutoring session — 91
Figure 9.1 Abby teaching a class — 100

Table

Table 8.1 Elements to consider in an ESL classroom observation — 88

Acknowledgments

First and foremost, I acknowledge the work of the adult English learners, graduate students and TESOL teachers who contributed their stories, so I could create the narratives presented in this book. I hope to honor their journeys and efforts learning and teaching a second language. I trust that I have been true to their stories by creating narratives that inform and inspire other learners and teachers.

Another group of people I would like to acknowledge is the many mentors in my career in adult English as a second/foreign language in Colombia, Puerto Rico and the USA. My success as a teacher educator, adult educator and researcher is due in large measure to their guidance and teachings.

Finally, I thank my family for their understanding and support. *¡Querida familia, aunque estemos lejos, siempre están en mi corazón y los amo mucho!*

*I'm thanking you, G*OD*, from a full heart,*
I'm writing the book on your wonders.
I'm whistling, laughing, and jumping for joy;
I'm singing your song, High God. (Psalm 9 (1–2))

Te alabaré, Señor, con todo mi corazón.
Contaré todas tus maravillas.
Me alegraré y me regocijaré en ti;
cantaré a tu nombre, Altísimo. (Salmo 9 (1–2))

1 Introduction and Supporting Theories

Narratives of ESL Learners and Teachers

The focus of the book is on language pedagogy useful to graduate students and practitioners in the fields of adult education, adult literacy and English as a Second Language (ESL), regardless of their teaching experiences (e.g. novice, experienced teachers). Specific sections of the book address relevant topics such as setting learning goals, assisting students to enjoy reading, forming strategies to move students from oral language to print, boosting adult learners' confidence and ESL student motivations to mention a few. Through storytelling, the author presents her point of view and invites the reader to reflect on their beliefs and practices regarding adult learning and teaching.

What sets this book apart is its overarching focus on language pedagogy and a humanistic approach to adult literacy development and ESL learning and teaching. The book presents language as functional and interactive, as a tool to express ideas and accomplish goals for having a satisfying life. Through language individuals create and maintain relationships with other human beings, even if they do not share the same point of view on a topic. Thus, language serves as a tool to develop human capital and participate in democracy. Through language, people negotiate and request services and express satisfaction or dissatisfaction to advocate for civil rights and human rights. When teaching a language, then, the focus should be on educating the whole person and envisioning the learners from an assets point of view. In this way, the focus is on their strengths and talents rather than their flaws or deficiencies. Therefore, the nurturing and creation of human relationships are of crucial importance in Teaching English to Speakers of Other Languages (TESOL).

The main goal of this book is to honor the work of language learners and TESOL practitioners and to share highlights from their journeys. This book can benefit advanced undergraduate and graduate students majoring in TESOL as well as instructors and practitioners in the fields of Adult Education, Adult Literacy and English as Second or Foreign Language. When planning for the content and format of this book, the need to rely on the wisdom of adult learners and practitioners and place their learning journeys at the center of this book became evident. The narratives come from actual English learners, teacher-learners and practitioners with whom I have collaborated on several projects. The data utilized to build the different case studies presented in this book come from different research projects examining literacy and TESOL instruction and learning.

Book Content

Each chapter has the same sections, starting with an, explanation of main concepts, stories narrated by learners and teachers, conclusion, recommendations for practice, and discussion questions. An appendix with relevant terms and acronyms utilized throughout the book appears at the end followed by a list of references cited in the different chapters. The theory supporting the case studies is interwoven in the content of each chapter to illustrate the connection between theory (abstract knowledge) and practical application (classroom). In addition, the cases are split into two parts: Part 1 presents learners' voices in Chapters 2–5; and Part 2 presents teachers' voices in Chapters 6–9. None of the names of people or places that appear in this book are real names. This conforms to the confidentiality agreement between the researcher and the participants in the narratives.

Learners' voices

Chapter 2 highlights Alberto, who struggled with reading because he believed it was boring and made him fall asleep. His story illustrates the point that adults can, in fact, discover that reading is an integral but fun part of an adult's daily routine. Chapter 3 describes the case of Doña Inés and provides suggestions on how to assist adults with low literacy skills to engage in learning and participation. Chapter 4 addresses the case of a group of parents learning by using intergenerational reading practices. It illustrates how these practices can boost adults' confidence to use English to communicate in public. Chapter 5 presents two case studies documenting adult learners' motivations for attending ESL classes through community-based programs. Their narratives reveal motivations unique to their identities and individual stories as immigrants and learners.

Teachers' voices

Through narratives provided by Janet, Sarah and Mary, Chapter 6 describes the work of two religious organizations offering ESL and literacy instruction to immigrants. The chapter describes an ESL program housed at a Catholic Church and a federally funded refugee program run by a religious organization. Chapter 7 posits public libraries as learning spaces that benefit all types of adults in the community and promote the development of literate communities. Here, Daisy, an ESL and GED (General Education Development) instructor, librarian and coordinator of adult education programs at a public library, shares her point of view. Chapter 8 illustrates an engaged scholarship approach to training ESOL teacher-learners. It portrays the learning experiences of ESOL teacher-learners and their reflections participating in observation, tutoring, conversation and internship as teacher-training events. Chapter 9 narrates the story of Abby, an experienced ESL instructor. It presents her work setting and a description of how she negotiates the curriculum to develop trusting and caring relationships with adult learners.

Conclusion chapter

Chapter 10 briefly summarizes the content of the different chapters and discusses the emergent themes from the case studies presented in this book. Then it addresses theoretical connections, suggestions for future research and concluding thoughts.

Conceptual Framework

More research documenting how second languages are learned/acquired, the factors that influence this process, and effective teaching practices to teach ESL and literacy to adults is still needed. Therefore, the author situates this book in a conceptual framework that views teaching and research as shaped by engaged scholarship, Freirean pedagogy, and second language acquisition theory. This framework informs the author's beliefs that:

(1) Teaching, research, and service are interconnected practices. Constant and reciprocal collaboration for learning should be established between university instruction and the community education needs.
(2) Critical reflection and dialogue are crucial to learning and the professional socialization of ESOL teacher-learners.
(3) Second language acquisition theory serves as a lens to present the narratives of English learners and TESOL instructors as case studies worthy of consideration.
(4) L2 is both learned and acquired, but learners and teachers should center on language acquisition practices. Communication should be the focus for learning and teaching a language.
(5) Students should participate in learning activities that promote the acquisition of knowledge first-hand through projects and direct contact with the communities outside the classroom.

Engaged scholarship

Engaged scholarship requires university faculty to create a reciprocal partnership with the community. It is interdisciplinary and integrates teaching, research and service (Boyer, 1990, 1996). The practice of engaged scholarship requires a basic reconceptualization of university faculty involvement in community-based work (O'Meara & Rice, 2005). It invites faculty to make the conscious decision to look for opportunities to work with local communities, to take the students out of the classroom to apply their learning in the real world where theory becomes relevant (Boyer, 1996; Lebeau & Bennion, 2014; Udall *et al.*, 2015). This is then a call for collaborative research, where all participants have a voice and find benefits.

Engaged scholarship entails the collaboration between academics and individuals outside the academy for the mutually beneficial exchange of knowledge and resources in a context of partnership and reciprocity (Boyer, 1996; Elwell & Bean, 2001; Lebeau & Bennion, 2014; Udall *et al.*, 2015). More than just providing a service to the community, through engaged scholarship, university students gain knowledge and benefit from learning with and from community members such as TESOL instructors who are more experienced and their adult learners. These are learning experiences that cannot be provided by just discussing theory in the university classroom (Udall *et al.*, 2015). The participation of non-academics enhances and broadens involvement and consideration about major social issues inside and outside the university, such as the literacy and ESL education for adults in the local communities.

Specifically, as illustrated in this book, the practice of engaged scholarship opens doors to work with community-based organizations dedicated to serving immigrants and economically disadvantaged adults and families in need of ESL and literacy instruction. In training TESOL instructors, all university courses should have at least one assignment in which they interact, learn and provide a service to the adult learners in the community. Through participation in engaged scholarship projects, graduate students acquire practical knowledge that they could simply not have access to by staying confined in the university classroom (Elwell & Bean, 2001; Udall *et al.*, 2015). The goals should be to create, support and document possibilities for change informed by community members and their actual needs. In this way, researching partners (i.e. practitioners in the community and their learners) can inform and dictate what is best for their learning and teaching contexts.

Freirean pedagogy

Utilizing a Freirean approach to research and teaching allows focus on real issues in the lives of adult English learners and their families (Freire, 1970). In such an approach, pedagogy is a process that focuses on individual learners as they interact within a social context and within a specific community (their work environments, neighborhoods, cities, their children's schools, etc.). In listening to the learners, the teacher learns to speak with them (Freire, 1998: 106). Through dialogue, teacher and learner engage in identifying problems, asking questions and developing strategies for transformation. Freire (1998) argued that listening is a permanent attitude on the part of those involved in dialogue and implies 'being open to the word of the other, the gesture of the other, and the differences of the other' (1998: 107). Thus, listening is a requirement for successful dialogue. Freire (1998) reminded educators and learners that true listening does not diminish the right to disagree, to oppose or to take a position. Thus, dialogue is a means for teachers and learners to communicate and learn from each other. They 'can speak engagedly and passionately about their own ideas and conditions precisely because they are able to listen' (Freire, 1998: 107). Freire envisioned learning as a never-ending activity giving purpose to human existence. He equally believed that teaching and learning are inseparable: 'Teaching, which is really inseparable from learning, is of its very nature a joyful experience' (Freire, 1998: 125). He described education as a 'situation where the teacher and the students *both* have to be learners, *both* have to be cognitive subjects' (Freire, 1987: 33). In this view, teachers and learners are required to keep an open mind and become active participants in learning.

As exemplified in this book, when teaching adult English learners and training TESOL instructors, dialogue takes the form of critical reflection and collegial conversation. The role of the teacher is that of an equal partner who engages in dialogue with learners in the spirit of democratic inquiry and solidarity (Freire, 1970). Through keeping a reflective journal and discussing learning, university students identified new learning, pointed out areas for improvement, asked questions and pondered solutions to education issues and social problems. As Freire (1970) stated, 'The word is more than just an instrument which makes dialogue possible ... Within the word we find two dimensions, reflection and action ... A true word is to transform the world' (1970: 87). The written and spoken word were the tools for the instructor, learners and practitioners to communicate with each other. In this two-way meaningful dialogue, we constructed and reconstructed reality together in the university classroom and the reflection journal served as a springboard to talk as academic individuals and as people. This dialogue was based on reflection, negotiation of ideas and communication. This practice allowed for discussion and conversation about issues selected by the teacher-learners and topics relevant to them.

Second language acquisition

Second language acquisition (SLA) is the study of how second languages are learned and the factors that influence this process (Moss &

Ross-Feldman, 2003). SLA research focuses on 'the developing knowledge and use of a language by individuals who already know at least one other language' (Spada & Lightbown, 2010: 108). SLA is a complex process involving a wide range of factors such as the learner's characteristics and experiences, the social and cultural environment, the structure of both L1 and L2, opportunities to practice with L2 speakers, access to form-focused instruction and constructive feedback (Lightbown & Spada, 2013: 212). In addition, Brown (2000) claims that the process of SLA is influenced by the learner's cognitive skills and personality type, involves L2 culture learning, language interference, interlanguage and the learning of communicative functions. In summary, SLA research examines how communicative competence develops in a second language (Savignon, 1997). Communicative competence is the ability to interpret the underlying meaning of a message, understand cultural nuances, use strategies to avoid communication breaking down and apply grammar rules in an organic, natural manner (Moss & Ross-Feldman, 2003).

There is not a single best method to teach/learn a second language; instructors are rather encouraged to adapt and borrow from the different methods what makes sense to the conditions of their classrooms (Ellis, 2010; Larsen-Freeman & Anderson, 2011). However, many have favored a communicative approach to language teaching and learning. In communicative language teaching, the goal is to develop the ability to communicate in the target language (Savignon, 1997); grammar learning is important, but it is not as important as developing fluency to communicate (Bax, 2003). Communicative language teaching encourages learners to incorporate their personal experiences into language learning; the focus is on the learning experience as well as language learning (Nunan, 1991). For the language learning experience to be meaningful, students should be able to establish connections to their real lives, goals and aspirations, and learning needs.

A pioneer in SLA research, Krashen (1985) proposed a series of hypotheses to guide the understanding of the language learning process: (a) the acquisition–learning distinction; (b) the natural order hypothesis; (c) the monitor hypothesis; (d) the input hypothesis; and (e) the affective filter hypothesis.

First, the acquisition–learning distinction hypothesis (Krashen, 2009: 10) explains that language acquisition is a subconscious process. However, learning is a conscious process and refers to knowing the rules of how language works, being aware of them, and being able to talk about them. Second, the natural order hypothesis suggests that the acquisition of grammatical structures proceeds in a predictable order. Learners tend to acquire certain grammatical structures early and others later (Krashen, 2009: 12). Third, the monitor hypothesis speaks to the learner's ability to autocorrect language production. Krashen (2009: 15–20) explains that the learner would need to have time to make self-corrections, focus on form or think about how to self-correct mistakes and know the rule for self-correction to happen. Regarding the input hypothesis, Krashen (2009: 20–30) states that people acquire language when they understand the input (i) and when presented with a challenge ($i + 1$), which is possible using context, prior knowledge and extra-linguistic information. Lastly, the affective filter hypothesis (Krashen, 2009: 30–32) explains how affective variables (e.g. motivation, self-confidence, and anxiety) relate to the SLA process.

Even though Krashen's work has been crucial in the discussion of how second languages are learned, the input hypothesis has been widely criticized by researchers in the field based on the vagueness of the construct, the simplification of input and the overclaims that he has made about the hypothesis (Liu, 2015). For example, Ellis and Fellow (2008) stated that 'contrary to Krashen's insistence that acquisition is dependent entirely on comprehensible input, researchers now acknowledge that learner output also plays a part in second language acquisition' (2008: 4). Similarly, other authors (e.g. Gregg, 1984; McLaughlin, 1987; White, 1987) have criticized the comprehensible input hypothesis for lacking a precise definition, leaving room for different interpretations of what $i + 1$ means, and for not providing solid evidence of how the input hypothesis works.

Case Study Method

A case study is a research approach in which detailed consideration is given to the development of a person, group or situation over a period of time. Case study involves 'in-depth investigation of the meanings that individuals ascribe to a particular phenomenon, known as the cases, in their natural setting' (Gall *et al.*, 2010: 344). The case should describe a problem that piques the reader's curiosity and that provides space for interpretation so that the reader can think of alternative solutions. In this context, a problem refers to a complex situation where different events play out at the same time such as adult immigrants learning ESL within the context of the United States. Accordingly, a case study approach encourages collaboration with study participants and contains enough information for the readers to be able to identify the issue or issues at hand. Merriam (2009) explains that, in a case study, the reader can experience a feeling or understanding relative to the person or people at the center of the study. That life-sense or feeling will be projected for the reader as they become familiar with the participant in the case study.

A 'case study is defined by interest in individual cases … It draws attention to the question of what specifically can be learned from the single case' (Stake, 1994: 236). Therefore, the different chapters of this book focus on a specific group of learners within a particular teaching context. The research setting is Texas (USA) and includes the organizations and programs where the learners and teachers described in this book have participated in learning and teaching English. Creswell (2013) explains that:

> Case study research is a qualitative approach in which the investigator explores a real life, contemporary bounded system (a case) or multiple bounded systems (cases) over time, through detailed, in-depth data collection involving multiple sources of information (e.g. observations, interviews, audiovisual material, and documents and reports), and reports a case description and case themes. (2013: 97)

Thus, the case studies presented in this book are anchored in real-life situations and provide a rich and holistic account of the narratives of adult English learners and instructors. The chapters in this book focus on individual cases and describe groups of people who have experienced the same phenomenon related to ESL learning and teaching.

In telling the stories of ESL learners, ESOL teacher-learners and practitioners presented in this book, different themes emerged and are discussed in the different chapters as they become relevant. Therefore, the focus is on practical application and constructivist research to derive knowledge that can be shared with others. The data collection sources to build the different case studies included audio-recorded conversations and in-depth interviews, artifacts, observations, reflective journals and field notes (Creswell, 2013; Merriam, 2009; Patton, 2015). Thus, corroboration of results through different data sources and several stages of analysis ensured the consistency of findings presented in this book (Patton, 2002; Rossman & Rallis, 2003; Yin, 2009). The different data sources collected are brought to life through the narratives of learners and teachers as they reflected on their teaching–learning experiences.

Instrumental case study

The instrumental case study is utilized to document and explore ESL teaching–learning practices. As Stake (2005) explains, here the case itself is secondary to providing insight into 'something else'. In the different chapters of this book, the case study method served as the catalyst to report on the results of different qualitative research projects implemented to document the state of ESL teaching and learning and to gain understanding on the efforts of different organizations providing ESL instruction. The different cases presented in the book provide insight into the challenges and successes associated with adult ESL teaching–learning practices. Then, case study methodology assisted the author in drawing conclusions relevant to adult learners, practitioners and other professionals interested in TESOL and literacy issues.

Narrative

Narrative is the primary way human beings order their experiences and make sense out of seemingly unrelated events (Worth, 2008). In this book, storytelling and narrative are utilized to interpret, manage and report findings from data collected to write the different chapters (cases). According to Wajnryb (2003: 8–12), experience is the raw material of story; Wajnryb explains that story moves from the individual, introspective domain to the social, more public domain and emerges as a narrative text.

According to Wajnryb (2003: 10–12), it all starts with an experience (an event or happening). Next, it moves to a story (the event as reflected upon), which constitutes the individual's perception of what happened. Then it becomes a narrative text (the event as represented), which is the social domain; the story is made available to others. Thus, case studies depicted in this book utilize short, true stories as told by English learners and TESOL instructors with first-hand experience in language learning and teaching. In this regard, their narratives appear in first person in the effort to give voice to the learners and teachers' lived experiences (Merriam, 2009). The end goal is to convey clarity and applicability from the ideas and findings from each case study for readers to transfer and apply.

In addition, Reissman (2008) explains that narrative analysis connects events into a sequence that is consequential for action and for the meaning that the speaker wants listeners to take away from the story (2008: 42). The chapters and their respective stories contain a beginning, middle and ending. The beginning provides the context and supporting theory, the middle presents the main issue(s) to be considered and the end gives closure to the reader.

Analysis of narratives

The first step in the data analysis process was to convert all data into text by transcribing them. The next step was to read the transcripts of data collected from conversations, interviews, artifacts, observations, reflective journals and field notes to conduct open coding by making notes on the margins to identify emerging patterns and themes (Creswell, 2007). In addition, narrative analysis procedures as outlined by Taylor-Powell and Renner (2003) were helpful to approach the analysis through five overarching steps:

(1) getting to know the data by doing multiple readings of the data collected;
(2) focusing the analysis either looking at the research question, topic, time period, event, or case;
(3) categorizing the information by identifying substantive categories based on ideas, concepts, and/or behaviors from participants;
(4) identifying patterns and connections within and between categories by writing a descriptive summary for each category;
(5) interpreting the data to bring it all together, where the researcher examines the meaning, importance and lessons revealed by the data.

Throughout the implementation of these data analysis steps, inductive and deductive analysis processes were utilized. Inductive analysis refers to the 'immersion in the details and specifics of the data to discover important patterns, themes, and interrelationships; it begins by exploring, then confirming findings; guided by analytical principles rather than rules; and ends with a creative synthesis' (Patton, 2002: 41). The inductive analysis approach allowed the researcher to be open minded and discover what the participants in the different case studies wanted to transmit to her and the audience (the people reading this book). Inductive analysis was helpful to come up with patterns, categories and themes without presupposing in advance what the emergent themes would be.

Furthermore, before beginning the data collection process, 'deductive analysis requires the specification of main variables and the statement of a research hypothesis based on a theoretical framework for understanding specific observations or cases' (Patton, 2002: 56). Deductive analysis took place when using a framework with predetermined categories. The formulated framework encompassed three theories (e.g. engaged scholarship, Freirean pedagogy and second language acquisition theory). These theories served as filters for data analysis and as a guide to write up the case studies presented through students' voices and teachers' voices.

Patton (2002) explains that the inductive approach can be used to reveal patterns and categories towards the beginning of a research project while the deductive approach can be used to verify these patterns against an established set of defined rules or framework to explain the observations. Creating some of the chapters/cases involved using a specific theory (e.g. engaged scholarship, Freirean pedagogy and second language acquisition theory). However, hypotheses were not established ahead of time, but rather, the cases presented in the book aimed to illustrate what can be learned from students and teachers engaged in TESOL practices.

As Creswell (2013) states, 'the inductive-deductive logic process means that the qualitative researcher uses complex reasoning skills throughout the process of research' (2013: 45). There are many sides to a story and different factors influence the process of adult language learning and teaching. In interpreting and reporting the stories shared by learners and teachers, the researcher/author used both processes to make sense of these stories and build the respective narratives.

Narrative research in TESOL

Utilizing a storytelling approach or narrative approach to reporting findings from studying ESOL teacher's practice and learners' experiences learning language is not a new idea. However, this specialized body of literature is still evolving and becoming more popular among qualitative researchers interested in studying the L2 teaching/learning phenomenon. For example, Barkhuizen (2014) presents a timeline mapping out the literature relevant to this area of research starting in 1977 and ending with the most recently published research in 2014. This timeline organizes the existent body of literature into three categories: (1) language teachers' professional development and practices; (2) language learners' learning and language use; and (3) primary approach to analysis. Barkhuizen (2014) speculates that 'experimenting with new forms of analysis and reporting will mean that researchers will by necessity pay increased attention to relationships between narrative form, content and context' (2014: 452) while conducting narrative research in language teaching and learning.

Likewise, Barkhuizen (2007: 232) describes a narrative approach to exploring context in language teaching and makes emphasis on three crucial elements to create the narrative. These are: (1) the participants in the story – their own experiences and their interactions with others; (2) the time during which the story takes place, including its temporal connections to history and the future; and (3) the physical settings or places in which the story is located. Barkhuizen (2007) further explains that 'any story is positioned within the matrix or space that these three interrelated dimensions create, and it is within this context that the story is understood, by both the teller of the story and the narrative researcher' (2007: 232). Accordingly, each chapter in this book provides a detailed description of these three dimensions of the narratives to make them accessible to the readers.

Going beyond the three dimensions of narrative explained above (e.g. participants, time, and setting), Barkhuizen (2011) argues that 'the preparation of narrative research texts involves further meaning making, as does the reception of these. [He refers] to this multistage, active meaning making as *narrative knowledging*' (2011: 393). In other words, the researcher collects the stories, interprets them, constructs new narratives and shares these findings with an audience that in turn will assign new meanings to the narratives. As Barkhuizen (2011) puts it, '*Narrative knowledging* is the meaning making, learning, or knowledge construction that takes place during the narrative research activities of (co) constructing narratives, analyzing narratives, reporting the findings, and reading/watching/listening to research reports' (2011: 395). He further explains narrative knowledging as a multi-stage, cognitive activity in which people make sense of and re- shape an experience through narrating, analyzing narratives, reporting narrative research and consuming research findings (Barkhuizen, 2011: 396). It is these many stages of meaning making which favor learning from reflecting on one's and others' teaching practices.

The book author agrees with Barkhuizen (2007) that a narrative approach to exploring one's teaching practice leads to a better understanding of that context and hopefully sharing this learning will promote change and encourage other teachers to make sense of and reflect on their personal teaching stories. In fact, Barkhuizen (2014) posits, 'narrative research in language teaching and learning is concerned with the stories teachers and learners tell about their lived experiences. Teachers typically tell about their professional development and their practices, and learners about their experiences of learning and using languages' (Barkhuizen, 2014: 450). This explanation thoroughly describes what the present book aims to accomplish.

Conclusion

This chapter briefly introduced the main theories supporting the case studies presented throughout the book. The intention in sharing the discussion of these theories in the introductory chapter is to facilitate the flow of ideas and concepts while reading the case studies in the subsequent chapters. Thus, the different cases will be presented in a smooth narrative form for the teachers and learners' stories to be easy to follow and only relevant literature to each specific case will be discussed in the chapters. Following the conclusion, the reader will find a section with recommendations for practice. These are pieces of advice related to best TESOL practices. Finally, the discussion questions section attempts to invite the readers to engage in meaningful reflection and conversations with colleagues.

Recommendations for Practice

(1) Read more about engaged scholarship theory and identify a community-based project you can implement. Think of collaborations and collaborators who you could work with towards promote change in the local community, regardless of how small these changes are.
(2) Make a list of resources you have available. These include, but should not be limited to material goods, people, technology, physical infrastructure and possible volunteers willing to participate.
(3) Identify a couple of theories of language learning and teaching that reflect your professional values and beliefs. Use these ideas to explain how you envision TESOL and/or literacy instruction.

Discussion Questions (Group Activity)

(1) Which of the theories presented in this introductory chapter was new to you? How could you apply them in your continued learning?
(2) Which theories were familiar to you? What do you see as other relevant theories? Explain and provide examples.
(3) Besides what was mentioned in this chapter, what are other uses for case study method in education?
(4) How do you envision SLA? From your personal/professional experience, what factors influence second language learning and acquisition?

Part 1
Learners' Voices

2 Learning to Enjoy Reading in ESL

Community-based Programs

All of the case studies presented in this book are embedded in community-based programs. Therefore, it makes sense to address the concepts of 'community' and 'community-based education' here in this chapter. For example, Galbraith (1990) suggests that individuals in the United States live in a *megacommunity* that is international, national and local in scope and defines *megacommunity* as a 'large scale systematic community that is connected by cultural, social, psychological, economic, political, environmental, and technological elements' (1990: 8). Within the context of the United States we need to view community as a *megacommunity* so that adult education services support the intellectual, human and social development of all its residents.

Furthermore, community-based education refers to programs providing adults with learning opportunities on a specific issue they believe to be important in improving life in the community (Merriam *et al.*, 2007). These programs can be described as a geographically bonded concept in which local access to instruction influences learners' decision and ability to participate (Neville *et al.*, 2014: 51). To this effect, community-based adult education instruction and training are often offered free of charge to facilitate access and provide services to a wider range of adults. Community-based programs involve a variety of settings, such as community centers, the workplace, colleges and universities, private adult education programs, literacy and ESL programs, public schools, religious settings, military bases, banks or financial services offices, libraries, non-profit, cooperative agencies, government buildings and homeless shelters (Tisdell *et al.*, 2010).

A study conducted by Neville *et al.* (2014: 52–53) documented the impact of community education and the benefits of participation in adult community education to include the following: (a) gaining personal development and confidence that positively impact relationships with family members; (b) creating and sustaining social support networks for themselves; (c) developing an informed social awareness for political activism and empowered relationships with social institutions; (d) developing self-confidence to interact with professionals and statutory agencies to offer opinions (to individuals and agencies); and (e) feeling empowered to continue learning. In other words, community-based education offers adults the opportunity to become more knowledgeable and competent in their skills, attitudes, beliefs and world concepts with the end goal of creating a better life for themselves, their families and society. Through participation in community-based education, adults gain skills and confidence for increased human capital and democratic participation.

Setting ESL Learning Goals for the Term

Working as a volunteer ESL instructor at a literacy center in Texas that offered four levels of ESL, I taught intermediate or English level 3. Alberto was 24 years old at that time. He emigrated from Mexico at age 17 and had nine years of formal schooling in his country of origin. He worked as a carpenter and lived with relatives. While enrolled in this course, Alberto missed class only once because he had a cold. He was the youngest person in class and had been attending ESL classes in this program for a year and a half. This was his third time taking the course. In his words:

> Every new teacher used to ask: 'What do you want to learn?' but it never went farther than that. They usually forgot about what we had said, but not you ... Every time that class begins, you ask: 'Announcements anyone? How about your learning goals?' That makes class different because nobody knows what we are going to tell; it might be good or bad news, or what is going to happen in class with a new topic proposed by someone different each time, and you follow through! (Alberto).

At this adult literacy center, one of the monthly required class activities was to ask students to fill out a form to outline their goals to learn English. Even though all instructors fulfilled this requirement, there was not a follow-up plan to monitor these goals or to re-evaluate them and establish new ones. Each month, students filled out a form provided by the center entitled *Student Monthly Goals*; the instructors collected the forms and delivered them to the program coordinator. Thus, Alberto was expecting the new instructor to ask him about his learning goals for the class and for them to be forgotten after that. However, he received a copy of the form and he could use it through the month to monitor and focus on his learning goals.

At the beginning of the following class, the students received a copy of their goals and applied the concept of 'SMART' goals. This acronym stands for 'specific, measurable, attainable, relevant and time bound' goals. A quick Google search will provide worksheets and further explanation on how to design SMART goals. Helping students to establish clear learning goals and commit to attainable goals is important in increasing learner motivation and retention (Bello, 2000; Moss & Ross-Feldman, 2003). Often students do not have experience setting learning goals, and they are either too ambitious, too general or too abstract about what they want to learn. For example, Alberto's first attempt at setting a goal was, 'I want to improve my English'. Once he and the instructor discussed and practiced designing goals, they became SMART goals:

> I want to improve my reading skills by reading in English outside of class. My plan is to read for at least an hour on Saturday and Sunday every week this month. I will use reading strategies and I will read something interesting, so I am motivated to read. I will report to class and will keep a record of the times I did sit down to read during the weekend.

The second attempt to set his learning goals for the month illustrates all of the components established by the SMART goals concept. Alberto's goals became more specific than just 'wanting to improve my English'. He established a plan of action explaining how and when he would work on achieving his goal of improving his reading skills. This goal was relevant to him since he had been in the program for a year and a half, and he became more aware of his lack of reading comprehension and fluency when reading in English. In setting his goal for the month, he also identified segments of time when he would be able to work on achieving his goal. Finally, he specified what his accountability measure would be, 'I will report to class and will keep record of the times I did sit down to read during the weekend'.

In class, every week, the students reviewed their goals to report on what they had accomplished and re-evaluated the goals to examine what was not working or why the goal was not being met. As an extra step, the class celebrated accomplishments for continual motivation towards the end goal: becoming fluent and achieving an advanced language performance for real-life purposes and to see themselves as literate adults.

Reading is Boring

In a journal entry for class, Alberto shared his feelings about reading, 'I'm not good reader ... It's boring. I sleep when read much ... I prefer movies'. Then, he asked the teacher, 'How did you learn English? At the beginning when you didn't know anything ...'. Her answer was, 'I used to read a lot. I started reading short stories. Those stories that are labeled by the number of words. I started with books of 200 words, and then, little by little, I increased the number of words'. Alberto did not know about these books or that he could get them at different bookstores and the library, and his teacher volunteered to help him find these books.

The next time class met, during the announcements segment, Alberto received a book as a present from the teacher. He looked surprised and

18 Part 1: Learners' Voices

excited to receive the book; it was *The Kingdom of the Golden Dragon* by Isabel Allende. Alberto explained, 'I had not read an entire book before, but I feel pressure to read this book now'.

During class activities when telling stories about the different cultures represented in the classroom, Alberto shared about Mexico and the legends that he believed were important to him from a cultural point of view. For example, he told the story behind the coat of arms of Mexico which illustrates the legend of Tenochtitlan. Below is a picture of a Mexican coin that Alberto brought to class to illustrate this story (see Figure 2.1). The coat of arms of Mexico is an important symbol of the Mexican culture. It shows a golden eagle standing on a prickly pear cactus eating a rattlesnake. In the legend, this image has a strong religious connection. Alberto explained that 'the eagle represents the sun god, the cactus represents the island Tenochtitlan, and the snake represents wisdom'.

Similarly, the plot of *The Kingdom of the Golden Dragon* is set in the Forbidden Kingdom, a remote Himalayan country. The main characters go on an expedition to locate the Golden Dragon, a sacred statue and priceless oracle that can foretell the future of the kingdom. In this journey, the main characters must use the transcendent power of their totemic animal spirits, Jaguar and Eagle, to fight and protect the holy rule of the Golden Dragon. Clearly, this book could be interesting for Alberto because the fantastic plays an integral role in Allende's writing. Her characters are real, and their lives, although accented by magic and spirits, are easy to relate to. The hope was that Alberto could relate to the characters in the book.

Figure 2.1 Photo of a Mexican coin provided by Alberto

In the class journal entry for the following week, he wrote: 'I promis I will read the golden dragon book, maybe not all but at least half'. He thought the expectation was to report on his reading and progress, but the idea was for him to practice reading for pleasure, the reading people do on their own, when they do not have to report to anyone, and as literate adults who read for pleasure or because they have a genuine interest in it. They may discuss the reading with a friend or colleague as an informal activity to socialize, not as part of an assignment.

Since no one else in class was reading this book, and Alberto never reported about the status of this reading to the whole class, he would volunteer to report to the teacher informally. During the break or after class, he would tell her about the plot and his opinion about the events in the book. She listened to him and shared what she enjoyed about the book. She did not ask reading-comprehension questions and treated him as a friend or colleague who had read the same piece of literature. Two months later, Alberto was surprised to report that he was almost finished reading the whole book. He was able to make cultural connections to the fantastic stories in the book and to the main character. To this effect, Mason (2006) suggests that 'an obvious way to promote student learning autonomy is to introduce them to free voluntary reading, a pleasurable activity that students can certainly do on their own' (2006: 2). This was a practice encouraged by Mason (2006) when training English learners to pass the standardized test that was the focus of the course he was teaching.

Those in favor of free voluntary reading or reading for pleasure (Abdullah *et al.*, 2012; Krashen, 1988, 2003; Mason, 2006, 2017) believe that it is the most powerful tool in language education. This type of reading is 'an effective way of increasing literacy and language development, with a strong impact on reading comprehension, vocabulary, grammar, and writing' (Krashen, 2003: 15). In class, once a week, the students practiced silent reading for half an hour and everyone in class was required to bring something they wanted to read during that time. Once the 30 minutes were over, the students took turns to talk about something they enjoyed about the reading they did or something they were puzzled about. There was not an answer-question activity, and everybody was reading what they wanted to read. The instructor also sat to read to model this practice for the students. The goal was for them to envision reading as an activity that could be just for pleasure, to have a conversation with others, and a social activity to be enjoyed, not just homework.

The students brought a variety of reading materials such as comics, the newspaper, specialized magazines and books. They also kept a tally sheet with dates and titles of what they had read during the month. They would bring it to class at the end of the month and share it in small groups to let each other know about the readings they had enjoyed the most or when they accomplished reading an entire journal article, a chapter in a book or a whole book. This practice motivated them to read outside of class and gave them an opportunity to have conversations about their own reading. Abdullah *et al.* (2012) believe that, when students engage in reading for pleasure, they develop a positive attitude towards reading. Mason (2017) also argues that students who experience reading for pleasure continue reading for fun even after their English course is over. Those who do more recreational reading show better development in reading, writing, grammar and vocabulary (Krashen, 1988). The course instructor hoped that the learners would realize that 30 minutes of reading could go a long way in the process of learning a language.

Reading for Pleasure

Adults want learning to be purposeful, practical, relevant and immediately applicable (Mackeracher, 2004). As a case in point, when asked about when they read in English outside of class, the students provided very interesting answers. For instance, Alberto reported that, 'I read in the afternoon, when looking in the newspaper for new movies, or when looking for a job ... or car ... *ventas*? [sales] And when helping a friend to find used cars. He buys them, repairs them, and then resells them'. Asking this question helped Alberto and other students in class realize that they do reading outside the classroom and that reading has many purposes and looks different depending on those purposes. Alberto wrote in his journal 'reading is boring, I cannot concentrate, and I fall asleep'. However, during class discussion, he also stated that he liked doing reading for specific purposes and to help friends. He was excited when he reported this. The instructor emphasized that this was important reading and that adults do a lot of reading in their daily lives and work routines. Once she said this, Alberto and other students in class were able to see the value of the reading they did outside of class and that reading is not just sitting to read a whole book. At first, the students thought that reading was only for academic purposes.

An important point for ESL instructors to keep in mind is that adult learners bring with them an array of life experiences, skills and talents, language proficiencies and learning experiences, often neglected in the classroom practice – their funds of knowledge. The concept 'funds of knowledge' is an approach to curriculum development and teaching that has been explored in the K–12 curriculum; however, authors such as Zanoni (2007) and Larrotta and Serrano (2011) believe that this concept is also relevant when teaching ESL to adult learners. 'Funds of knowledge' refers to the bodies of knowledge developed socially and historically by Latina/o households (González *et al.*, 2005). It includes a positive view of households as containing ample cultural and cognitive resources that can be utilized for classroom instruction (Vélez-Ibáñez & Greenberg, 1992).

In addition, Larrotta and Serrano (2011) found that adult learners' funds of knowledge include the student's personal stories, their learning motivation and goals, perseverance and resilience in learning the language, the extracurricular activities and strategies that they use to learn and communicate in English, and the learner's point of view, attitudes, values and inquiries about language. Thus, it is important to validate the learning activities that students practice outside the classroom. In this case, they may feel encouraged to continue reading, practicing and learning English even after class hours.

Connecting Students' Lives with Classroom Work

In this ESL 3 class, the instructor implemented a project called *Inquiry cycles*. The goal of the project was to practice asking questions and reading outside the classroom to find answers to these questions. In this case, inquiry is a process initiated by the students in which they investigate central, essential questions while their instructor guides them through the process (Short *et al.*, 1996). To start, there was a mini-lesson on how to formulate questions and with the help of the students, there was consensus on what 'a good question' was. A good question connected to the student's life; it was interesting for the student to invest time researching answers and it fostered English learning. Then, as a group, the class formulated examples of acceptable questions and individually the students formulated the questions they wanted to use for the activity. As a next step, students received assistance to identify the information sources to use, such as the Internet, books or key people to interview to gather information relevant in finding answers to the questions they had formulated for their individual projects.

In summary, steps for implementation included: formulating the question, identifying sources of information, doing a preliminary report of progress, performing an oral presentation with a poster and coming up with the next inquiry question to start a new cycle (Larrotta, 2007). Alberto explained that the inquiry cycles project 'is not the traditional assignment. There is no repetition, and it is interesting because it's new; it's a different way of learning ... we choose a topic of our personal interest. Nobody imposed on us the topic to investigate'. In implementing the inquiry cycles project, Alberto and his classmates realized that reading could be beneficial and interesting:

> My question for this class project was: Why is there racism in the U.S.? Doing this project, I have learned English and other things such as reading can be interesting. I didn't know all those things that happened with the Martin Luther King Jr. movement, for instance, or the problem of racism in this country. That's why I liked the inquiry project and because it's different from other activities I have done in other classes ... it's like a challenge and I can decide what to read and when.

By asking everyday life questions, student motivation and investment in learning English increased (Larrotta, 2007). The inquiry cycle project implemented in Alberto's class promoted reading as a tool to find information and learn English. A good amount of incidental learning took place during the implementation of this project.

Incidental learning refers to the unintentional learning or unplanned learning that results from other activities that adults do. It occurs in many ways including observation, repetition, social interaction and problem solving (Kerka, 2000). To complete the inquiry cycle project, Alberto and his classmates were reading with a specific purpose in mind. He wanted to find answers to his question and information that could help him report findings to the class. He was reading from books and the internet, and he was not aware of the amount of reading he was doing. Reading was no longer a passive activity or boring. Alberto was able to make a personal connection to reading, and he was able to understand that reading is not boring or a tedious task if he reads to find out about a topic he is interested in learning about. This and other projects that involve reading as a secondary activity or reading to accomplish a task can be helpful in changing student perception about the role of reading and its usefulness. Overall, reading activities served as an anchor to develop and practice other language skills such as speaking, listening, writing and learning about culture.

Reading to find answers about 'why there is racism in the U.S.', Alberto practiced writing by taking notes for the oral report he was going to present in class. He also learned history and the civil rights movement. He discovered the importance of Martin Luther King Jr as an iconic figure in US culture and the civil rights movement. Alberto and his classmates practiced listening when their classmates presented their projects in class. They also practiced speaking when they presented and interacted to discuss and present their projects.

Alberto Fails the Test

At the end of the term, all of the students were pulled out of class one by one to be tested for progress. Alberto was very familiar with the evaluation system at the literacy center and had taken the same standardized test for the last year and a half. Alberto confessed that he sometimes provided incorrect answers while taking the test to fail it on purpose and be able to stay enrolled longer in the literacy program. As mentioned before, the literacy center only offered four ESL courses (levels 1–4). Once they passed the exam, the students were promoted to the next course level, and after passing the exam at the end of level 4, they were to exit the program.

Because the students enrolled as many times as necessary in the same ESL level until they passed the standardized test, Alberto was attending ESL 3 for the third time. While the instructor noted a significant improvement in his reading comprehension and writing skills, the test results did not reflect these improvements. When asked about the exam results, he explained that he had failed the test on purpose; it was a common practice among his classmates to be able to stay enrolled longer in the program. The program coordinator was not aware of this situation. There was a need for the center to start offering a conversation class and a computer class to provide extra practice for the students. However, there was an issue with the lack of space and instructors to be able to offer more classes. They still had to test the learners every four months to show scores for funding purposes. This center was fully run by volunteers. Only the program director and program coordinator were employed full-time and received a salary. The rest of the instructors and staff were unpaid volunteer instructors.

Conclusion

Using a case study approach, the chapter presented Alberto's ESL learning journey focusing on reading skills and providing glimpses into his personal story striving to become fluent in English. The chapter briefly explains the main class activities implemented in this course and focused on Alberto to provide examples of how these activities impacted student learning. It also provides narratives describing the different facets of Alberto's journey learning ESL. Specifically, Alberto developed a more positive point of view about reading.

Reading is an important language skill that all adult learners need to develop regardless of their language level. It is through the practice of reading that students acquire new vocabulary and grammar through incidental (unconscious) learning. Students come to the ESL class with misconceptions about reading such as 'reading is boring'. The instructor can help these learners realize that reading is interesting and has many purposes. The instructor can do this by investigating and promoting the reading activities that the students do outside of class, reading for pleasure, and by exposing them to different reading genres and reading activities.

Recommendations for Practice

(1) Design and implement projects that involve reading outside of class.
(2) Provide students with opportunities to read for different purposes.
(3) Ask students about the times when they read in English outside of class. Explain in class why this reading is important and what they could be learning when reading outside of class.
(4) Do silent reading, peer reading, group reading and other reading activities in class.
(5) Read about the benefits of reading for pleasure and share this information with your students.

Discussion Questions (Group Activity)

(1) Besides giving a book as a present, what else can the TESOL instructor do to promote student reading outside of class?
(2) How can instructors help their students learn to enjoy reading?
(3) How can instructors utilize the Internet and social media to promote student reading?
(4) What is the role of prior knowledge and cultural awareness when assisting students like Alberto appreciate the value of reading?
(5) What do you read in your free time and why?

3 ESL Adults Transitioning from Oral Language to Print

Dialogue and Storytelling

The project described here was a literacy class for parents offered once a week during the evening as part of a partnership with a local public elementary school. The class was designed to involve Spanish-speaking parents in learning and practicing reading strategies that could benefit their children. Therefore, the goal was to promote intergenerational literacy practices at home. The parents attending the literacy class were expected to read at home with their children and practice the literacy strategy we had studied together that week. During class time, there was a lecture on the steps to implement a particular reading strategy followed by practice working in small groups and practice with the whole class. The adult students practiced a reading strategy with each other to be able to do it at home with their children. Every week, they wrote a journal entry reporting and reflecting on how the home practice went. This journal was also used for students to write a response to the reading that was explored during class time.

I was the class instructor for a 10-week after school literacy class to teach parents and adults from the community surrounding the school. We met once a week for two hours, and 17 adult learners (ages 27–65 years old) enrolled in the class. They all spoke Spanish as their native language and all of them were from Central and South American countries (e.g. Mexico, Honduras, Colombia and Venezuela). The narratives presented in this chapter come from data collected through interviews, class records and field notes, the students' class journals and other writing assignments.

The focal participant for this chapter is Doña Inés, a 65-year-old learner. She started as a quiet student who rarely participated and struggled a lot with class activities involving reading and writing. However, when the instructor brought culturally relevant readings to class, she blossomed and became an active class participant. Doña Inés was able to participate in discussions and storytelling at the oral level but moving from oral language to print was a challenge for her.

Dialogic practices and storytelling served as umbrella concepts to deliver the class. Dialogue 'is the encounter between [people], mediated by the word in order to name the world' (Freire, 1970: 69). It is through dialogue and conversation that we arrive at a consensus and learn from each other. Dialogue allows us to enter the worldview of the learners. Without dialogue, there is no communication, and without communication there can be no true education (Freire, 1970). In a dialogic classroom, students are able to express their thoughts and needs and the teacher listens and learns about the students' reality. Likewise, learning through stories involves listening to stories, telling stories and recognizing the elements in a story (Clark & Rossiter, 2008). Through storytelling, the learner becomes an active participant; teacher and learner build collaboration and support each other in the teaching–learning process. Of course, stories must be received and interpreted; 'they engage the learner's cognitive skills, spirit, imagination, and heart' (Clark & Rossiter, 2008: 65). In fact, the adult learners enrolled in the class were highly motivated to engage in dialogue and reading comprehension strategies when the topic was highly familiar to them and when they felt personally connected to those topics. Congruent with existent research, study findings point to the value of stories in teaching and learning. For example, Rossiter (2002: 1) explains that narrative is deeply appealing and richly satisfying to the human soul.

In the telling of stories, the learner becomes the actor rather than the receiver; the learner moves from a cognitive understanding of a concept to linking it to their own experience, and new learning occurs. Both dialogue and storytelling are helpful tools when working with adult learners who have low literacy skills. In addition, several elements of this case study can be cross-referenced with the concepts and ideals outlined by the study of funds of knowledge. Oughton (2010) explains that funds of knowledge represent a positive and realistic view of the cultural and cognitive resources available within the households of underprivileged or struggling citizens. Funds of knowledge therefore can provide a direct and positive influence for members of these families to acquire a strong education. The students use what is familiar to them, their skills and talents to acquire new knowledge.

Teaching the Teacher: Doña Inés Blossoms

Doña is a courtesy title used before the name of a woman in Spanish-speaking countries. It is also a Spanish title equivalent to *Mrs* or *Madam* to show respect. Doña Inés was a Mexican female student at least 10 years older than her ESL instructor, who was from Colombia, South America, and grew up aware of the importance of showing respect to her elders.

Her age reminded the instructor that Doña Inés had more knowledge and life experience. She had lived longer, and culturally the expectation was to learn from her wisdom. Therefore, it is crucial to refer to her as Doña Inés while telling her story in this chapter. In addition, she taught her ESL instructor a lot during this ESL class. For example, she taught her about the importance of the *agave* plant and recipes to prepare *nopales* (cactus), and she made her reflect on the importance of the decisions made when planning a lesson. Doña Inés called the instructor 'maestra' (teacher) and that was her way of showing respect as well.

Doña Inés was the typical adult learner with low literacy skills in her native language but aware of the importance of learning English to participate in US society. She was a homemaker attending ESL classes, overwhelmed with caring for her three children and husband, and with little formal education. In class, when there was a writing activity, she would hold her pencil and look at the blank page for a while. When asked how she was doing, she would provide the answer or tell her teacher what she wanted to write. Sometimes, the teacher would ask her to tell what she wanted to say, and she would write it down for her, so she could have a chance to express her opinion and participate in the group activities. Writing was difficult for Doña Inés because she was not a fluent writer in Spanish, her native language. Back in Mexico, she had only attended school up to fith grade. This made her shy in class, and she would be quiet most of the time when the class was discussing a reading or when they were practicing writing in the class dialogue journal.

Building on learners' knowledge

A body of literature on reading discusses the role of background knowledge in facilitating reading development in ESL learners (e.g. Coatney, 2006; Peregoy & Boyle, 2005; Singhal, 2005). According to Singhal (2005) the reader's factual knowledge, cultural values, understanding of the organization and purpose of a written text, and ability to recognize words and their relationships to each other in a sentence all affect the ability to comprehend a written text. However, this may prove challenging to the instructor when the native language foundations of the adult learner are not strong either, as in the case of Doña Inés. Writing was not a daily practice for her and her classmates. An alternative solution to approach this issue is to motivate learners to write by utilizing compelling topics to read and write in class. To build on background knowledge the instructor selects texts on familiar subjects and then shares stories and uses pictures and graphics to bring learners into the text through their own experiences (Coatney, 2006). This strategy allows the learners to make connections with print and to feel capable of participating in class activities that go beyond oral language.

Compare and contrast

One of the reading strategies studied in class was 'compare and contrast', and, for this strategy, the instructor selected a reading about different types of *nopales* (cacti). It seemed appropriate to implement the compare and contrast literacy strategy and it was a one-page reading with easy to understand vocabulary. It looked like a simple reading to cover in one night and focus on the literacy strategy at hand. However, the students from Mexico, Doña Inés in particular, knew a lot about *nopales* and the cultural relevance of *nopales*. The teacher's knowledge of *nopales* was limited; in Colombia this is considered an ornamental plant. However, the students spoke about it being edible and delicious and that it could be transformed into an alcoholic drink called 'tequila'. This is how, when reading and discussing about the agave plant, Doña Inés would sound like an expert, and her oral language fluency transformed:

> I come from the Agave Region, in the Valley Region of Jalisco State [see Figure 3.1]. This reading reminded me of my youth in Mexico harvesting agave ... I grew up in a big ranch where we cultivated the agave plant to transform it into tequila. Seven steps are involved in the production of tequila: Harvesting, cooking, fermentation, distillation, aging, and bottling. The planting, tending and harvesting of the agave plant requires manual labor, it is a labor of love ... it is almost like an art ... and it's passed down from generation to generation.
>
> I feel nostalgic when I remember those years of my life at the ranch back in my country. It reminded me of my Mexican roots. It also made me feel sorry for my children because they have not experience this love of the simple life ... the life at the ranch!
>
> Remembering my past life at the ranch I can breathe the air, the peace and quiet of the countryside ...

Figure 3.1 Image of agave plantation provided by Doña Inés

The ESL teacher did not have much knowledge about *nopales*, the *agave plant* or tequila. When she selected the reading for class practice, the focus was on how to teach a reading strategy. Through her students, she learned that agave was part of the Mexican national identity and vital to the economic development of Jalisco, a large state in Mexico. Doña Inés and her classmates from Mexico knew all about *nopales* and tequila and taught the class about the many recipes and processes to transform this plant into food or liquor.

Doña Inés found the needed confidence to participate in class discussions and to share her knowledge with the rest of the group. Clark and Rossiter (2008) explain that 'good stories transport us away from the present moment, sometimes even to another level of consciousness. They evoke other experiences we've had, and those experiences become real again' (2008: 65). Reading about cultural and familiar topics like *nopales* did this to Doña Inés. Her eyes would look off in the distance, and she would use sophisticated language to express herself at the oral level. The class would go quiet and listen to her with admiration. She made a few mistakes but none which would cause communication breakdown. The teacher did not interrupt her and would only ask questions to learn more about her experience and to have her gain confidence to continue to participate in class.

Moving from Oral Language to Print

Learners need to make connections between the words and structures they are reading and their own realities in the world (Coatney, 2006). In the class, bringing information and artifacts from places where the learners lived and worked was helpful to motivate them to write. Similarly, storytelling provided room for meaning making and inspired authentic writing. For example, Doña Inés shared with the class her culinary talents and she wrote recipes and cooked some of them to share with her classmates and teacher. As she would say, 'With the prickly pear juice you can make jam, candy, cocktails, or vinaigrettes for salads'. In her journal entry for class she wrote:

> The prickly pear have tiny pointy-hair
> to handle them wear heavy work ~~globes~~ gloves.
> Scrub the prickly pear hard
> Remove thorns.
> The pulp – the fruit is inside the pear.
> Cut and discard both ends of the prickly pear
> Make vertical cut to ~~peal~~ peel it off.
> Don't eat the skin. That you don't eat.
> Now put the pulp in the blender.
> Pour the juice through the strainer.
> Discard pulp and ~~sids~~ seeds
> It looks like much work. but it's easy to do ☺
> Inés

This journal entry was Doña Inés' response to the class reading about *nopales*. For a student who rarely wrote much, this was a lengthy journal entry in which she described a recipe on how to use the *nopales* fruit to extract the juice and make a vinaigrette for salads. When asked about the process of writing the recipe, she explained that this was her third draft. She wrote the sentences to explain the process using separate paper, consulted the dictionary for spelling and asked her son for some of the words she used. In the last version, with the strikethrough words, she also let the class know how she self-corrected her writing for the spelling of words that she was unsure about and that she consulted in the dictionary.

Recipes use precise language and new learning happens through using recipes. For instance, Doña Inés uses expressions and verbs such as scrub, remove, discard, make a vertical cut and pour. These may be language pieces that she would not normally use in a conversation, but this language fits perfectly well within the context of sharing a recipe. It was an engaging learning activity where she practiced spelling and writing via a recipe. Through recipes, students learn ingredient names, specific verbs and the language to interpret and tell about the steps involved in a recipe. Even though it looks like a simple exercise, writing a recipe motivated Doña Inés to be engaged in the writing process. It was an authentic activity with a purpose and an audience in mind. Her purpose was to share knowledge she already had to an audience of classmates and a teacher.

In moving from oral language to print, Doña Inés and the other students in class were able to construct poems, write letters, prepare poster presentations and keep a personal journal. Throughout the term, Doña Inés became a more confident learner and shared her knowledge with enthusiasm. For example, she read her poem aloud. The class video recorded these poems so that the students could share them with their children and family members at home. Doña Inés also started to volunteer more often to read her journal entries in class in the group-sharing segment of the lesson.

Extending the lesson

By utilizing storytelling and culturally appropriate readings and homework, the literacy class became more than just a meeting for learning English. It became a welcoming space to share knowledge and connect with one another while having a common goal in mind: studying English and reading strategies. The teacher provided the students a template with the beginning of sentences that they could use to describe themselves and write a poem: an autobiographical poem. Below is a typed version of the poem that Doña Inés wrote for class:

I am a neighbor of the city of Austin.
I live in a yellow house on Main Street.

I have three children.
I love them too much.
I feel proud to be Mexican and a mother.
I'm afraid of loneliness and not being able to protect my children.
I like the color blue.
I want to learn English just fine.
My name is Inés.

Writing and sharing the poem for class was a collaborative activity. There were two or three drafts before the final version was read to the entire class. The students read the poem to each other while working in pairs and rehearsed it to be ready when the camera started rolling. Recording the poem to share it with people at home gave the students the appropriate motivation to work on this activity. There was a lot of chaos in class, but everybody was on task. Once the video-recording started, everybody listened quietly and clapped when people were finished reading the poem. It became a class event!

Keeping a class journal was another way to help students practice writing weekly. The journal was an individual, private writing activity and a space to practice writing fluency. The students decided when they wanted to share it with the instructor or the whole group. The following journal entry is a letter that Doña Inés wrote to her 10-year-old son Daniel:

Dear Daniel, Mi Amor.
I write to you today because I want you to know how much love I have for you.
I only want the best for you. I want you to study.
I am in this class to give you example.
It is important to study.
I want you to be a engineer, a doctor, a teacher.
Whatever you want but not a beggar like the one we saw yesterday at the park.
I know you are rebelious and I am old but I love you.
I want my best for you.
With love, Tu mamá, Inés :)

Daniel was Doña Inés' youngest son, and he was not doing well at school. The letter she wrote for him is testament of the love she feels for her son. It is also a message she wants to transmit to him to do better at school because education could be a window for success. The students in class wrote the letters and put them in envelopes to then hand deliver to the person that they were addressed to. Doña Inés reported that her son got emotional and gave her a hug when he received her letter. They had a conversation, and he promised to put more effort into his studies. These letters were a success in the ESL class. Doña Inés and the other students in class worked hard to write their messages and were invested in the activity. They did at least one draft and consulted with each other, the instructor and the dictionary to have a nice product to deliver.

Supporting Adults with Low Literacy Skills

The research presented in this chapter adds to a growing body of scholarship that focuses on how adults with emergent literacy skills approach language learning and the learning strategies that could benefit them. They may respond differently than adults with well-established literacy skills to daily routines of classroom learning that require print literacy (Burt *et al.*, 2008). Therefore, the instructor needs to be a good observer and follow the students' lead. In the case of Doña Inés and the other students in class, they were familiar with the Roman alphabet, and that was helpful. Even though her level of schooling was at the fifth grade level, she was a great story teller and was committed to learning. The ESL instructor drew on those strengths to plan the lessons and class activities. In class, she did activities such as copying from the board or copying from a reading, dictation and reading aloud. She built on simple activities to increase the level of challenge for class purposes. Each student was able to work and learn at his/her own pace, and they supported each other through cooperative work by working in small groups and as a whole class group. The class celebrated accomplishments and encouraged each other to become more confident in using the language in reading, writing and sharing in public.

One activity that was challenging for all but useful was to present the learners with a scrambled sentences exercise. The instructor would pick a story and cut it into strips to separate the different sentences in the story; then she would put it in envelopes to distribute it in class. The students would rearrange the sentences in the proper sequence to be able to read the complete story. This activity was helpful in teaching the parts of a story and recognizing key phrases in those parts. The students were able to discuss and arrive at a consensus in order to rearrange the story to follow a sequence that made sense to them. An extension activity was to write a reader's response in the form of a letter, poem, recipe, a different ending, a newspaper commentary, etc.

The selection of class materials was also an important step. The ESL instructor made sure to provide the learners with flashcards, photographs, magazines, video cameras or a disposable camera, short poems, crossword puzzles and markers and big paper. These are materials that allow support for low literacy-level students to have a tactile experience and visual aids to support the transition from oral language to print. They also support the development of fluency, vocabulary building and reading comprehension, which are three important areas for students to develop when they are at the low literacy level. For example, in this class the students played picture dictation; using blue tape, the teacher would paste photographs on the walls of the classroom with a number under them. Next, she would divide the class into pairs; one person had to stay sitting down and write what their partner whispered. The person standing had to describe the photograph as accurately as possible. Then, at the end, those sitting had the opportunity to see how accurate their written description was. As a class, the students voted on who had the most accurate description to win a prize (usually chocolate or cookies). This activity was seen as a game, but it helped students with fluency and vocabulary building. The students had fun and they were learning while doing it.

Conclusion

The after-school ESL Literacy project provided the learners with space to experiment with literacy learning and to use dialogue and storytelling as bridges to move from oral language to print. The learners developed confidence and shared their expertise with their peers and teacher. They were able to establish connections to their immediate daily lives and learning needs while striving to develop English literacy skills. Adult and community educators as well as their learners can benefit from potent learning experiences when engaging in similar practices. It is imperative that literacy instructors realize the benefits that can occur when they provide room for students to tell their own stories and to put these stories into writing.

In helping adult learners with low literacy skills, the instructor should provide plenty of opportunities for the learners to practice the steps of the writing process. In other words, they need to be able to work on several drafts to have a final product. They should also write with an audience in mind. The audience can be the teacher and the classmates, but it is also important to include people from outside of class (e.g. family members, their children's schoolteachers or a service provider). This way the students will be able to appreciate the usefulness of preparing several drafts and implementing the writing process.

Recommendations for Practice

(1) Be flexible and create opportunities to learn from your students.
(2) Allow students to shine and be the center of the teaching–learning process.
(3) Listen and reflect on what literacy activity to do next to capture your students' attention.
(4) Pick readings that bring to life the cultural flavors and traditions of your students.
(5) Read more on how adults with low literacy skills learn.

Discussion Questions (Group Activity)

(1) Have you ever been in a situation when you learned from your students? Share this experience with your colleagues.
(2) What can be learned from listening to the personal stories of adults with low literacy skills?
(3) What can instructors do to help students flourish within the constraints of the classroom and to transition from oral language to print?
(4) What would you learn from asking your learners to keep a reflection journal?
(5) What benefits do you anticipate from keeping a reflective journal?

4 Adults Building Confidence Through Family Literacy

Intergenerational Reading

In intergenerational reading, two generations or more participate in literacy activities (see Figure 4.1). Adults and children partner in literacy development and engage in reciprocal learning (Cooter, 2006; Gadsen, 2000; Packard, 2001). The advantages of implementing intergenerational literacy practices are many, and the focus is often on how they benefit children (Cutspec, 2004; Jimenez et al., 2006; Zevenbergen & Whitehurst, 2003). However, this chapter focuses on the benefits that intergenerational literacy practices bring to the participating adult. The adults involved in the project noted in their reflection journals that:

Alma: These practices are very important because they help me in having knowledge on how I can help my child and I can explain parts of the reading to help him understand. With the strategies that we are being taught it is much easier to practice the readings and it makes reading fun for us.

Isabel: At the beginning I didn't take into consideration what I was reading. There are several steps to follow; I have learned that when we are reading we are learning something new. Everything I learned helps me to keep practicing with my four daughters, and through studying we will all have a better future.

Josue: Last week my wife and I worked on our project to build the poster for *The Seven Ways to Fill an Empty Bag*. Today I presented the poster with my son. First, I felt nervous because I'm shy but then, later I felt more relaxed. When I practiced with my child I felt good because we talk and arrive to a consensus.

Alma, Isabel and Josue explain the value they discovered in utilizing reading strategies. Practicing with their children, they were able to rediscover the value of reading. Reading together and implementing the strategies together (e.g. building a poster) encouraged them to discuss and plan together on how to explain the main points of a reading.

Figure 4.1 Maria and her children working together

The Reading Project

My name is Marla and I am Mexican, a good mother, sanguine and choleric, and how you say 'con muchas metas?' [Marla quickly flips out her phone to check for the translation of the phrase muttering to herself. Having found the meaning on the app on her phone she smiles to the audience and repeats] 'goal oriented', and I like cooking! I have three children. Two girls and one boy. My kids are Kayla, Jules and Joshua. They are 14, 12 and 5 years old. I came today because the coordinator said this class is to teach us to read for our kids. I want my kids, all, to go college. For me I want get better job. I also want to learn speaking English better and read and write better. I cook in restaurants for 9 years, but I quit since my hours no work with the time Joshua got out of school. Only my husband is working now, so I want to get a better paying job to add money to the family purse. I want a better life for me and my family.

The family reading project was a collaboration between a university faculty member, two research assistants, the school assistant principal, parents from the school and their teenage children. As Marla explains above, the focus of the family reading project was to promote bilingual, Spanish–English, pláticas/conversations among participants and practice intergenerational reading. We met for two hours during the evening for 10 weeks and used bilingual texts so that all participants in class had a chance to be a language expert. We read texts such as the bilingual edition of *The House on Mango Street* by Sandra Cisneros, 'The Healer/*La Curandera*' and 'Making Tamales/*Haciendo Tamales*' from the book *In my Family/En mi Familia* by Carmen Lomas Garza (1996). We read about personal finance and discussed three chapters from Suze Orman's (1998) book on 'The 9 Steps to Financial Freedom'. We also read fiction: *The Tell Tale Heart* by Edgar Allan Poe and the prologue to *El Manual del Guerrero de la Luz/Warrior of the Light: A Manual* by Paulo Coelho.

We practiced reading in different modalities such as group reading, reading aloud, silent reading and peer reading. We studied different reading comprehension strategies and the participants received bilingual Spanish–English handouts explaining the steps to implement these strategies. The parents kept a journal and reflected on their practice throughout the term. Two research assistants took field notes and I recorded the lessons to transcribe them later.

Setting and participants

The study started with an invitation from the assistant principal of a public middle school located in a rural area in Central Texas. Seventeen families (24 adult parents and 16 children) attended the family reading project. All of the participating parents were from Spanish-speaking countries such as Mexico, El Salvador, Honduras, Guatemala, Colombia, Venezuela and Peru, and their ages ranged from 27 to 45 years old. Their level of schooling was a variation of elementary to some high school and a college degree from their countries of origin. All of the participating children had attended elementary school in the United States and were enrolled in middle school. Most of the parents spoke English at the low intermediate proficiency level and were beginning ESL literacy learners. The children spoke Spanish as a heritage language but had difficulty reading and writing in Spanish. These teenagers' English skills were at the intermediate-advanced level, and they were still in the process of developing their academic English. The school assistant principal, John, served as the liaison to the school personnel and parents. I was the lead researcher and was immersed in the setting as a full participant teaching reading and writing to the families. Two graduate students played the role of research assistants and helped with answering questions and supporting the parents when the class broke into smaller groups to practice concepts or do group work. Parents sat with their children next to them, and they worked as a unit or team.

Building Confidence

Parents need to use English in the adult world at work, with the neighbors, when going shopping, visiting the doctor's office, communicating with their children's teachers and performing other tasks. In their interaction with other adults, they sometimes feel shy due to their accents or lack of language proficiency. They may feel doubtful and inadequate trying to accomplish a task that requires using English in public. The classroom is the appropriate place to assist them to develop this confidence and practice strategies that can help them in their daily activities outside of class.

Speaking on the phone

Performing authentic tasks in class such as practicing speaking on the telephone gave the parents confidence to use English. The parent would find a quiet place outside the classroom to call their child and speak in English about a task or class activity such as telling a family story related to the class reading we were exploring that evening, and the child would support the parent by listening and providing verbal responses as appropriate. The parents were required to tell stories that were new to the child to be able to pique their interest and to make the activity meaningful. In the beginning, there was confusion and hesitation, but gradually, the adult's confidence grew, and as a group, we addressed what was difficult or fun and we all laughed in the end. In their journals, the parents reported reactions to this activity:

> Sandra: Speaking on the phone is hard. It is hard not to see the other person and help them understand my message. Sometimes my child repeated words for me to make sure he got it right. That was helpful for both of us to avoid communication breakdown. Some other times we used words in Spanish too. But that was OK. That is what happens in real life at home anyways.
>
> Ignacio: Listening on the phone is not easy. My child has really good English. Her accent is good! It makes it difficult for me at times. Speaking on the phone you can't see the person's face and you don't know if they are following what you are saying. It gave me anxiety but at the end we laughed and my daughter got the story I wanted to tell her.

Making sure that parents and children were performing tasks that included elements of information gap was the key to make these phone calls authentic. Parents reported that this practice helped them later in real life situations to communicate with their children over the telephone and to make phone calls to speak to other people using the strategies for conversation that we rehearsed in class.

Practicing challenging words

Vocabulary development activities are a good way to help adult ESL learners build confidence in spelling and using what they call 'difficult words'. To get started with this idea, we created a vocabulary wall. During class, using index cards and markers, the learners wrote a favorite word and a difficult word for each of the participating family members and pasted them with blue tape on the left wall in the classroom. Next, they were paired up with another family and they explained what made the words challenging or favorites. Then, every family chose a word from the wall and a sentence of at least seven words that included the self-selected word. The research assistant and I circulated around the classroom to make sure the sentences where coherent and the vocabulary words were being used correctly. This and other similar exercises helped students lose the fear of challenging words (see Larrotta, 2011). This was an activity the parents could also do at home to study words they urgently needed to learn to accomplish a personal goal (e.g. speaking to their bosses or their child's schoolteachers). For example, Melba, a study participant, wrote in her journal:

> We have certainly been practicing at home and learning lots of new words and facts. My children are super interested in this class and every night they are ready and waiting for a new incomprehensible story. I say incomprehensible because that's how it feels at the beginning but after reading 2 or 3 times we start to ask questions and in the end we get answers and comprehend the story. Today my children and I worked on the story on Alligators and Crocodiles. We learned new things like that they are the only reptiles that have cold blood, that they live in sweet waters and that they both have a lot in common.

Another activity that worked well was to sing a song every three weeks, and practice singing the song for 15 minutes each time we met. This activity supported student listening, word retention and pronunciation once they identified challenging words. Through the songs they also learned about metaphors, improved their ability to connect words and grasp the rhythm of the language, talked about culture, and learned full expressions and phrases they could use in everyday conversation.

The same happened by practicing pair dictation – family A chose five words from a reading and dictated them to family B; then they switched roles taking dictation. The learners practiced words they liked or words they found difficult to spell and remember.

> This group dictation is a fun idea. It becomes a game, a competition. I think that is why my children like it. They want us to win the spelling game. They help me identify difficult words to dictate to the other family so they lose. (Josue's journal entry)

Here the parents and their children practiced spelling, pronunciation and writing. The children knew how to help their parents because these were activities familiar to them, and because they were competitive.

Reading with their children

Most parents reported that reading with their children in class and at home gave them an opportunity to discuss relationships among family members. In particular, the parents reported an improvement in communication with their children. In the reflection journal, they also shared how they felt about working with their children at home while practicing the reading strategies we studied in class.

Juan: The story of *Boys and Girls* from the House on Mango Street was something that my daughter understood perfectly. While we were reading I would tell her how this story is very similar to her and her sister. I told her she was Nenny [the sister of the main character in the story] and that her sister was the one that was speaking, Esperanza [the main character in the story]. Putting her in the story made it easy for her to understand the story. We talked about the relationship between her and her sister. She also understood the story *Pelos* [Hairs]. I just had to explain the last part of the story where the she compared the odor of the bread, the rain and the snoring. In the end I just gave her examples of what happens here at home.

Ismael: My son and I practiced reading the stories and I felt good in explaining what the story was about. I was able to understand what we were reading and I realized the importance of family getting involved in reading. We had a good conversation. As they grow I feel we do not talk as much anymore. This project gives us this chance.

Alba: We used the cubing strategy at home to read *Alligators and Crocodiles*. It was really helpful for my son to summarize the reading because it describes step-by-step how to make a synthesis that is good and can be understood. In only 6 steps you can gather the most important information pertaining to the reading. This is something my son can use with other readings. It was an easy way to do reading with him.

Practicing reading at home gave the parents the opportunity to interact and have dialogue with their children. The parents practiced the different steps involved in each reading strategy and they helped their children discuss what they grasped from the reading. Together they negotiated meaning and helped each other practice the language to create new learning.

Creating a storybook

The storybook was a class project we did, and parents and children created these stories together. First, we read short stories to help us identify the elements needed in a story (beginning, middle and end, plot, characters, actions, consequences, plot resolution). Next, we discussed and told other related stories. Then, students selected a topic and used disposable cameras to take pictures to accompany the stories. There was a limit of 10 pictures to keep focused on a self-selected topic for telling a family story. The school provided the funds to develop the pictures taken by the participating families. In class, we brainstormed for ideas looking at the photographs to start writing. We used class time for drafting and obtaining individualized feedback. During this time the children were very involved in helping the parents create the appropriate sentences to transmit the messages they wanted to convey as a family.

The families selected topics related to their cultural values, cultural customs, neighborhoods, homes, important family members, pets and children's adventures. They received help in class to polish their English and improve the stories in terms of content and coherence and each family wrote at least two drafts and a final version. They typed the stories in the school computer laboratory. The children typed the stories, and the parents dictated the sentences to them. We used a PowerPoint template to match the pictures to the paragraphs, made color copies of the PowerPoint slides and bound them to look like books. Finally, the families received their books printed in color, and they took turns to read their storybooks during the last day of class. As a result, the parents reported having developed a personal connection with writing and telling stories. They learned about word choice, sentence structure and the writing process (drafting, revising and publishing). Parents reported during class conversations that:

Jesus: I enjoyed the storybook activity a lot because it tells stories about my family and I am writing in English for my children. It helps me to think and practice writing in English. Reading the storybook in class was easy and fun. I wanted my children to hear me reading our story out loud to others in class.

Maria: I like the storybook activity because it's about my children and I really enjoy telling about them. They are my purpose in life and the reason for me to continue fighting for a better future. It is because of them that I have stayed here in the U.S. I want them to have better chances than what I had. This is why I volunteered to come to school and read my storybook at the faculty meeting.

Jesus and Maria's comments illustrate the importance of fostering confidence in the learners so that they are able to use English for communication purposes outside of the classroom. They represented two different families and they both volunteered to attend the school faculty to read their storybook to the teachers and school administrators. They wanted the project to be funded and offered by the school again so that other families could benefit. They were both proud of sharing their stories with the people at the school and were brave to do so. Selecting the topics to write the storybooks and writing about topics that were close to their hearts allowed for the parents to feel confident in reading these stories in public.

Doing poster presentations

While practicing reading comprehension strategies, the families were asked to create posters to present their understanding of a reading assigned to them by identifying the main idea and supporting details and using visuals such as drawing a diagram and actual pictures.

Parents and children read together to decide what was important in the story and to come up with a plan for their poster. They negotiated as a family how to design the poster and who would say what when they did the class presentation. We started in class, and they finished the poster at home. As a result, the families created posters of high quality using color, pictures and diagrams. I organized this activity as a poster presentation session similar to a conference. Half of the class presented their posters one evening and the other half presented the next night. All of the stories were different to make sure they all had an interest in listening to each other presenting their posters. Through creating poster presentations, the parents had another opportunity to practice public speaking. As illustrated below, the parents reported positive results on this activity:

> Ana: For me standing in front of others is truly difficult because I am timid and shy. I felt a little nervous. I would forget what is trying to say, I could not even read with being so nervous. I had to improvise and said half of what I planned to say. I can see the importance of the activity; it was challenging but made me feel good in the end.
>
> Luis: Listening to other parents do their presentations was encouraging. It gave me a good idea of how to do mine. It made me feel I could also do it. If they did good I can do good too or that is what I told myself. I saw older ladies doing a good job and I decided I could do a good job too. Why not?
>
> Rosa: Presenting with my daughter made my husband and I feel good. I want to be more secure as I do things and I want for my daughter and I to learn this step of presenting in front of others. I like this practice ... I like to listen to what others have to say because this way I learn different ways of saying it myself. We want our daughter to observe how her peers do it so that she can learn something new and have fun too. The three of us laughed and shared a lot working together on this project.

To develop self-confidence or the feeling of trust in their abilities to use language for real-life purposes, adult learners need to be exposed to authentic practice in the ESL classroom. Instructors need to prepare students for success; they must plan class activities step-by-step to guide the students and instill confidence in themselves. Once they experience success owing to a project's positive results, they will want to continue experiencing these positive feelings of accomplishment and being capable.

In addition, parents were able to connect with their children and learn together. They acquired strategies that could be used for language learning and for communication. During the last week of the course, I asked them to review the journal entries they wrote during the term and to reflect on where they were at the moment in terms of learning and the practice with their children. Thus, they wrote one last journal entry for our class:

Isabel: I read all my previous comments and I think that when I started this program I didn't have many strategies to teach my child. I did not have ways to read to him or ways to make it easier for him to understand. With the weeks of practicing the strategies that were taught it has been fun to read. Before this, reading didn't really catch his attention or mine. I didn't even like explaining to him, now I know how to have a conversation with him about what we read. Thanks for teaching all the strategies. Now I feel more capable of helping him with reading.

Maria: I feel happy reading with my daughter. I like the time we read. We connect more, we talk more. In the stories we try to find something to connect it to our daily lives. I like to talk to my daughters and my husband a lot because that helps us to live in harmony. When we talk we can know what is going on. If I don't talk with my daughters, I don't know what they are feeling or what is going on at school or if they need something.

It became evident that through their participation in the family literacy project the parents had acquired strategies on how to conduct a reading session with their children. They often reported knowing what to do to start a reading and how to explore the reading with their children. Another common feeling that they expressed was how they grew closer with their children again. Reading together allowed for them to have conversations and use reading as an excuse to talk. Therefore, the confidence they developed to communicate in English also transferred to communicating with their children.

Conclusion

Building confidence through intergenerational reading practices was possible because of the commitment and enthusiasm of the parents and children participating in this reading project. We practiced activities such as reading with children, speaking on the phone, learning vocabulary, creating a storybook and doing poster presentations. The parents and children found these activities useful and engaging because they were able to work together as a family to gain the needed confidence to express themselves in public. These adults acquired strategies to read, speak and present ideas in public. The children were able to assist their parents while relaying the academic skills that they had already acquired through attending school.

Boosting adult learners' confidence could seem like a difficult goal to accomplish but, with the appropriate class strategies and activities, it is possible. In Ismael's words: 'Some strategies were easier than others but now we have a list to choose from and can decide what works best. I feel more capable now to discuss reading with my child. I know what to do, how to start, what to do next, how to listen'. Learners need to acquire relevant tools for using language successfully.

Recommendations for Practice

(1) Keep in mind the characteristics of the learners to outline the appropriate strategies that will help them build confidence.
(2) Tackle language confidence development through different strategies and modalities (e.g. vocabulary learning, implementing reading strategies, public speaking practice, building relationships).
(3) Involve family members so that the students can practice at home.
(4) Trust that the students will outgrow their shyness and feelings of inadequacy using the language in front of a group.

Discussion Questions (Group Activity)

(1) Discuss why it is important to boost adult students' confidence using L2 to communicate with others in and out of the classroom.
(2) What other strategies can an instructor use to help adults build confidence using L2?
(3) What are the benefits of intergenerational reading practices for adult learners?
(4) How can the instructor use bilingual texts to promote reading and learner confidence?

5 Adult ESL Learners' Motivations

Motivation to Learn a Second Language

Motivation is the reason for people's actions; sometimes motivation comes from within the individual and other times from an external force. Motivation in a learning context refers to the drive to reduce uncertainty and meet unmet needs (Mackeracher, 2004: 132). The adult ESL learners' journeys presented in this chapter illustrate these definitions. This chapter discusses the learners' reasons behind their actions in attempting to master ESL and their desires and needs causing them to register in ESL classes repeatedly. The learners' stories revealed motivations that are unique to their identities and individual stories as immigrants and learners.

As Ellis (2008: 76) and Nayir (2017: 61) explained, motivation is dynamic in nature; it varies from one moment to the next depending on the learning context, the task in which the learner is engaging and how authentic this engagement is. Ushioda (2014) discussed a schematic framework further explaining this idea. She represented L2 motivation from a temporal perspective looking at the learner's motivation at different points in time (past, present, future). Ushioda's (2014) framework included (a) motivation deriving from past and ongoing experiences, (b) motivation directed towards future goals and (c) the process of L2 learning in a particular sociocultural environment. She explained, 'The overall motivational balance between cumulative experiential perspectives and goal-directed perspectives will vary from learner to learner and at different stages of L2 learning' (Ushioda, 2014: 129). Similarly, the learners described in this chapter will remind us that social and economic conditions can also have an impact on why and how adult learners' motivations to learn L2 change or evolve.

Gardner and Lambert (1972) considered the motivation to learn the language of the other community to be a primary force responsible for enhancing or hindering intercultural communication and affiliation. They discussed three psychological concepts to explain motivation to learn a second language or L2: (a) the learner's desires; (b) the learner's effort; and (c) the learner's attitude (Gardner & Lambert, 1972). From this perspective, the learner's motivation to learn L2 is driven by the willingness to learn the language (desire), the work that they put into learning (effort) and/or their approaches to learning the language (attitude).

Moreover, Gardner (1985) acknowledged two types of motivation to learn a second language: integrative motivation and instrumental motivation. In integrative motivation, the learner desires to learn the second language to communicate with community members to become immersed in the new community. In instrumental motivation, the learner has a functional goal in mind such as obtaining a better job. On the one hand, instrumental motivation refers to a practical or pragmatic reason for language study. Examples of instrumental motivations for language learning include passing a language requirement, getting a monetary reward such as an increase in pay grade for language competence or having a better chance of getting into medical school. On the other hand, integrative motivation suggests a positive disposition toward the L2 group and the desire to interact with members of that community. It implies openness and respect for the L2 cultural group and ways of life, and a certain level of psychological and emotional identification with the L2 group/culture.

In the same way, Ellis (2008) explained that 'motivation involves the attitudes and affective states that influence the degree of effort that learners make to learn an L2' (2008: 75). This researcher agrees with Gardner (1985) that L2 learners' motivation include integrative and instrumental motivation but added resultative and intrinsic motivation to the discussion as two more types of motivation to keep in mind. In resultative motivation, 'motivation is the *result* of learning ... learners who experience success in learning may become more, or in some contexts, less motivated to learn' (Ellis, 2008: 75–76). In relation to intrinsic motivation, Ellis (2008) suggested that 'motivation involves the arousal and maintenance of curiosity and can ebb and flow as a result of such factors as learners' interests and the extent to which they feel personally involved in learning activities' (2008: 76). When motivation comes from within (intrinsic motivation), the learners study L2 because they find it useful and enjoyable. Personal interest and enjoyment are associated with intrinsic motivation.

Likewise, Dörnyei (2003: 12–17) explained three research directions that have adopted a contextualization perspective to L2 motivation: (1) willingness to communicate; (2) task motivation; and (3) learners' use of language learning strategies. First, in willingness to communicate, the learner displays consistent tendencies in their predisposition toward or away from communicating in L2. This construct comprises several layers and subsumes a range of linguistic and psychological variables, including linguistic self-confidence; the desire to affiliate with a person; interpersonal motivation; intergroup attitudes, motivation and climate; parameters of the social situation; communicative competence and experience; and various personality traits. Second, regarding task motivation, tasks constitute the basic building blocks of classroom learning. The assumption is that tasks play an essential role in shaping learners' interest and enthusiasm toward learning. The quality of the activities used in language classes and the way these activities are presented and administered make a difference in students' attitudes toward learning. The third research direction related to the relationship between motivation and the use of language learning strategies. These are the techniques that students apply of their own free will to enhance the effectiveness of their learning. This is also addressed in the research as self-regulatory learning since it originates in learners' actions.

On this same line of thought, Dörnyei (2005) proposed an L2 motivational self-system which includes (a) the ideal L2 self, (b) the ought-to L2 self and (c) the L2 learning experience. First, the ideal L2 self relates to learners' aspirations, hopes and wishes. It represents a valued and cherished future possible self whose desirable attributes include L2 proficiency for personal, social or employment purposes. Second, the ought-to L2 self refers to the attributes that learners believe they must possess owing to obligations, responsibilities and expectations to avoid possible negative outcomes. It represents an externally imposed future image of oneself with a level of language proficiency shaped by the need to comply with expectations of others, bow to social pressures and demands, or avoid possible negative consequences. Third, the L2 learning experience refers to the role of prior learning experiences and the situated motives intrinsic to the immediate learning environment. Compared with the work of Gardner and Lambert (1972), Dörnyei's (2005) theory provides a more comprehensive view to explain L2 learners' motivations. Cognitive, affective and social aspects of the self are fundamental to his L2 motivational self-system theory.

In view of Dörnyei's (2005) L2 motivational self-system, the learners' determination to reduce the perceived discrepancy between the actual (here and now) self and a future L2 self provides the necessary motivation for language learning to occur. This notion then includes identity as an essential component of L2 motivation. Norton (2000, 2013) agreed with this concept linking motivation with learner identity, 'how a person understands his or her relationship to the world, how that relationship is constructed across time and space, and how the person understands possibilities for the future' (Norton, 2013: 45). Norton also argued that when the learners speak in L2 they organize and reorganize a sense of who they are and how they relate to the social world as 'an investment in the target language is also an investment in a learner's own identity, an identity which is constantly changing across time and space' (Norton, 2000: 11). In this chapter, this connection to L2 identity became evident through the individual stories presenting the motivations to learn L2 and the specific circumstances of the learners such as gender, age, familial relationships, geographical location and personal or employment and occupation goals.

The Adult ESL Learners

The narratives that appear in this chapter come from interviewing adult ESL learners attending two ESL classes, the conversation club at the public library and the ESL level 2 course at the Arboretum Learning Center (pseudonym) or ALC, an adult education center operated by a larger organization. The public library provided the space for adult learners from different ESL programs in the area to attend a conversation club. ALC offered ESL courses in the evenings for adults, and 80% of their students were male learners.

Semi-structured interviews, artifacts (photographs) provided by the learners and field notes served as data collection sources to craft the narratives on L2 motivations. The learners volunteered to share their stories and signed a consent form. Thus, three female learners (Viviana, Esperanza and Mariela) participating in the English conversation club and three male learners (Tito, Raul and Mauricio) attending ESL level 2 at ALC during the evening constitute the focal participants for this chapter.

Case Study 1: Learners Attending the English Conversation Club

Out of the 12 learners attending the conversation club, three volunteered to participate in the interviews: Viviana, Esperanza and Mariela. The goal of the conversation club was to offer the learners the opportunity to practice speaking English one-on-one with a native language speaker. The different ESL programs they attended during the long semesters (spring and fall) were closed for the summer and they saw an opportunity to continue their learning through the library English conversation club.

Viviana the nurse

Viviana was in her 60s (see Figure 5.1). She had moved to Texas from Guanajuato, Mexico at age 18 with no formal education. She was one of 14 siblings and began working at a young age to help her family.

> I was always so worried because I did not know English. If I stayed with my family and returned to Texas, I would never learn. I decided to tell my father I would not return. Oh, my father was very upset! When I worked in the field, I never saw money. It would all go to my father ... There was not many options in North Dakota. But I wanted a place where people did not speak Spanish. All my fears resume in not speaking English. I remember a man said 'good morning' to me while on the farm. I just ignored the man. I left to hide behind my brother. I let him talk. Without language and education, I was so limited.

Adult ESL Learners' Motivations   49

Figure 5.1 Viviana

After moving to the USA, Viviana worked with her brothers in the fields in North Dakota. For years, she worked on a sugar beet farm during season and would return to Texas during off-seasons. After finishing work in the sugar beets field one season, she decided not to return to live with her family. Viviana felt that she needed to learn English to help with her transition into having a life in the new country. Her family and current work environment did not require her to speak English; however, for someone who knew little English she progressed from working in the fields to operating machinery.

> I learned how to use the machine that piles the sugars beets by chance. The person operating the machine left me alone with it without telling me how to operate. I had to guess to first operate and luckily, nothing bad happened! To get better, I made a mock machine with buttons and levers and would practice at home. I enjoyed the job and was paid well for the time.

Later during the same year, Viviana obtained a job at a nursing home facility. She explained that her employers and her faith in God inspired her to look for a positive change. Her employers recognized that Viviana was a hard worker and could do more at the nursing home. They supported her to become a certified nurse and overcome the language barrier. In her words, 'The nursing home facility employer asked me to get a nursing certification to help more with patients'. While Viviana ran into challenges (e.g. financial, work and study, and language barrier), she was able to obtain her credentials and build a 22-year career, which she still performs today. Her determination to improve her life conditions motivated her to learn and overcome the language barrier. Realizing her potential and achieving her ideal L2 self were strong motivating forces for Viviana.

Esperanza the pastor

Esperanza was a 50-year-old pastor (see Figure 5.2) born in a small town in Mexico. The initial goal established at the beginning of the conversation hour was to practice English to build confidence when ministering. Esperanza's goal as a pastor was to have two services, one in Spanish and one in English. She was looking for other ESL programs available to her on a more formal level to continue working on this goal once the conversation program at the library finished. Thus, Esperanza seemed to be interested in continuing education opportunities. As she explained during the interview, she appeared to be self-driven and 'motivated as to master my calling to its highest capacity'. Esperanza displayed both self-motivation and self-determination throughout her life in spite of major obstacles and challenges.

At age 13, Esperanza knew of her calling to serve God in a specific way; therefore, she started and completed nursing school at an early age in Mexico. Married at the age of 20 to a minister, Esperanza served in ministry with her husband for several years. In 2016, she obtained her degree in Theological Studies. This was an 11-year process; she persevered in spite of major challenges such as her husband becoming terminally ill in 2015.

Esperanza's main motivation to learn English was her desire to connect with the English-speaking community at her church, or integrative motivation. Her congregation offered a fish fry once a month as a

Figure 5.2 Esperanza

community-wide initiative. In her words, 'This is a festive celebration of friendship and community. The community wide fish fry is a way to marry my Mexican culture with American food'. Esperanza also explained that she needed to make new friends and saw learning English as the avenue to achieve this goal. 'My husband became terminally ill in October of 2015. Since this time to current, I'm preparing mentally ... to live alone.' Her hospital trips to visit her husband became infrequent as part of her preparation to transition into a life without him. Esperanza expressed, with tears in her eyes, 'I know that the time is coming so I should start learning to live alone. He is still alive, but his death is coming.' Her reality of daily living and coping remained a challenge. The English classes she attended through church and the English conversation hour at the public library were her spaces to integrate to a new community and make new friends.

When discussing a photograph of her mother watching her receive the Theological Science degree, Esperanza expressed feelings of joy as well as sadness because her father was not there to witness that proud moment. Growing up, her father inspired her to be a life-long learner. He instilled in her that she could do anything. After such determination and drive, Esperanza became a pastor of a small Hispanic church in a small town in Central Texas. She frequently articulated how grateful she was to live in the USA as opposed to Mexico where she would have not been able to get this type of education. Esperanza was constantly seeking out opportunities to enhance her social skills to continue to contribute to her community and ministry work. Her identity as an immigrant, nurse, and pastor played an important role in fueling her desire to become a more fluent English speaker to communicate a message of service and to connect with her community members.

Mariela the clerk

Mariela, in her 60s, (see Figure 5.3) described herself as an ambitious, lovely and happy person. Her favorite activities were baking, knitting and learning. She had three adult children and five grandchildren and spoke frequently about them. Originally, from Laredo, Mexico, Mariela came to the USA with her family when she was six years old to live in Laredo, Texas because of her father's job. After her father finished his contract, they moved back to Mexico. At that point, she could read and write in English from what she had learned at school. However, her speaking skills had experienced a setback since that time as were hardly any occasions to practice English in her environment in Mexico.

At age 30 Mariela decided to come back to the USA. She worked at the Western Union in Laredo, Texas, for several years. In Laredo, she didn't need to speak in English since most of the people around her spoke Spanish. During the interview, she stated:

> My husband, who is fluent in English, would never help me practice and improve my English. It wasn't until I moved to Central Texas that I

Figure 5.3 Mariela

noticed the need to improve my English, specifically in terms of speaking. I started to work at Target store. Some of my coworkers and customers were not friendly because of my skin color. My lack of English was also a big problem in my communication with other people at work. The only nice person was my boss. My boss said that as long as I did the work, English did not matter. But communicating with people is the reason I enroll in the ESL Program. I don't have any American friends.

Mariela's motivation to attend the conversation club at the public library was primarily to communicate with others (e.g. her grandchildren's schoolteachers, her neighbors and other people outside her house) and become more helpful for her daughter and her grandchildren. The second reason was to better adapt to her new Central Texas community and work environment, and to make friends. When asked about friendship, she immediately said, 'I relate friends to cooking and eating, meeting for coffee and cookies, or converse'. Language was a barrier for her to build new friendships with neighbors and local people. She said, 'I don't have any American friends. I can't speak'. Thus, she decided it was time to participate in an ESL program offered at her church four days a week and the conversation hour at the public library to improve her English-speaking skills. Contrary to what she said, Mariela was able to communicate relevant information in conversational English. However, she felt the pressure to become more competent speaking English in her workplace. Reaching her ideal L2 self and her need to live up to the expectations of her co-workers and customers were important motivating forces for her.

Case Study 2: Learners Attending an Evening ESL Class

Seventeen learners were enrolled in ESL level 2 in this evening course offered at ALC. Tito, Raul and Mauricio were attending this class and volunteered to participate in the interviews. However, this section of the chapter focuses on Raul and Mauricio's stories and the input provided on their performance by their ESL instructors. Tito moved from Puerto Rico owing to a job offer. His story is incomplete because he stopped attending class after the third week and it was not possible to get hold of him to continue the interviews.

Tito moved to Texas

> I moved to Texas to work. I need to speak, write, and talk English every day. I started studied English last semester. I been living in Texas for two years now. I learn too much English last semester and I need to continue to improve. Being in class makes me feel motivated; the class is interesting; I lost the fear to speak English. Time run fast because it's fun. I am from Puerto Rico. I am a citizen, but English is not the everyday language in the Island. We learn it as a foreign language at school and I not payed attention then. It was not my need.

Tito saw learning English as a necessity because he had to use it every day at his new job in Texas. He found value in attending the ESL class to continue to learn the language. Tito had the right attitude and a strong instrumental motivation to learn English. There are many reasons why students stop attending ESL classes. During the first months when they move to the new community, they go through a period of adaptation as they find their bearings around the city and the new community. Tito may have moved closer to work and found another ESL center to continue learning the language.

Raul wanted to become a restaurant manager

Raul, a 30-year-old Salvadorian with an 11-year-old son, refused to speak Spanish from day one. He explained that his son was the reason for him wanting to build his language skills at an accelerated rate.

> Although I've lived in the United States for ten years, only two years ago I noticed that I was having trouble understanding my son when he spoke in English. My son has attending school in the local public-school system for several years and speak fluent English. When I started have trouble understanding him, I decided to increase evening classes to learn English ... I immersed in English ... only speaking in English from that point on. I work in a restaurant; they help me learning language ... the staff and

customers generally speak English. My co-workers understand this goal of speaking English with proficiency and encourage me by explaining what certain words and phrases mean.

Currently, Raul has not attained any formal education in the USA. His life dream was to become the manager of the restaurant where he worked (see Figure 5.4). Based on the data collected, it appeared that, to date, no one had suggested to Raul that pursuing his education could be an option to consider. Many instructors had tutored him at various sites across the city and at his work; however, no one had provided Raul with a list of options for a higher degree of education. He was unaware of the specific steps needed to earn a GED, how that could lead to attending college, a master's degree and beyond. Raul's instructor reported that:

> On the final day of class, we celebrated the time we spent together. Students gave presents to their teachers, and we gave them presents as well. I gave Raul a language book that focused on the use of irregular verbs. I also gave him a road map of formal education options. The map started with a GED exam and then progressed to enrolment at a two-year college, then a four-year college, a master's program and a Ph.D. I walked him through each of the steps with detail. This was the first time that anyone had walked him through these steps. Over the course of the last few weeks, Raul had expressed interest in attending some form of college. His eyes seemed to light up as I explained the potential road map of increasing formal education.

> Often others can see glimmers of our eventual path more clearly than we can. In the case of Raul, it is my suspicion that he may meet his goal of restaurant management. However, I also see a strong path in his life based on his character and industry that will lead him to fulfilment and accomplishment beyond his own conceptualization. Perhaps, the map to formal education options that I gave him, fuelled by his own character, determination, and imagination will begin to light the way to a life and dreams not yet realized.

Figure 5.4 Raul

It was important for the instructor to realize that Raul did not know about the steps to follow to earn a GED. The instructor was able to explain a systematic plan to pursue formal education. This could potentially influence Raul's future education goals. His instructor was able to recognize and fuel Raul's potential to continue to make progress and transition from ESL education toward GED and college. It became evident that Raul's motivation to learn L2 related to willingness to communicate with his son and at the workplace, the classroom environment and the instructors' support, as well as his expectations to grow personally and professionally. His desire to achieve his ideal L2 self and strong instrumental and integrative motivations to connect with his son and become a restaurant manager kept him motivated to learn L2.

Mauricio worked in construction

Mauricio was in his early 40s and worked in construction. Work was very important to him, as it was something he spoke about in each class and at each assignment (see Figure 5.5). His next passion was his family; he was married and had three children. Mauricio had lived in the USA for over 22 years and came from San Luis Potosí (Mexico). Reading aloud proved challenging for him; pronunciation was an issue because he had trouble recognizing some words. Often, he would know the words at the oral level but did not recognize them in writing.

Mauricio shared that, 'I enjoy learning English and play soccer. In this class, my goal is to work on everything, reading, writing, and speaking in English ... I also want to understand and be part of the American culture'. Mauricio was usually 15 minutes late for class; he would call to let the

Figure 5.5 Mauricio

instructor know about this; but he did not miss a class and was the last to leave. His work schedule made it difficult for him to be on time. Mauricio's instructor shared that:

> I showed two pictures of me while on vacation in Colorado. He lit up! He had many questions, such as how long it would take to drive there, where the snow was, and if I needed a guide to get there. This told me that his idea of Colorado, based on my pictures, was all about it being wild territory. The way he asked questions indicated that there was an interest on his part to potentially visit Colorado himself one day. When it came to learning about me and about Colorado, he readily asked more questions than when we were working on his reading. The following week Mauricio shared about having gone with his family to Six Flags over the weekend. This activity allowed me to get to know him better as a person.

Mauricio also shared some pictures he had taken from above his construction site. He wanted to know 'what scenery means and the words for all the trees and views in his pictures'. Mauricio knew that there was a particular vocabulary to express his thoughts about his work setting in construction, and he articulated the desire to develop this vocabulary. He brought a notebook in which he would write down words and their meanings in both English and Spanish. He also had his phone open to an English–Spanish dictionary application during class to help himself learn the meaning of words he did not understand. Mauricio explained that, 'I like when I find the solution, when nobody help me in Spanish. Because I can keep my mind more focus in talking and thinking in English'. Getting to know the personal stories of the students was fundamental to becoming familiar with the characteristics of the ESL learners and their motivations to learn. Mauricio's instructor reported:

> As Mauricio started to share his personal story, I could sense a bit of uneasiness on his part. I believe he was pondering how much he should divulge. Mauricio shared that he has been in the US on two different occasions. The first time, he came looking for adventure. He worked for his brother, who was a contractor for a small drywall installation company. Mauricio seemed somewhat regretful of his first stay in the U.S. He had an opportunity to learn English from attending school in the evenings. But he didn't take advantage of this because he was young and not thinking in terms of what skills he might need for the future.

In addition, Mauricio shared the following during the interview:

> Returning to Mexico, I met my wife. We came to the United States together and married here. My goal to make money to help my parents in Mexico. They still live there. We are close. I wish to take advantage of my opportunities to learn before. I did not take advantage to study English the first time. Now I really want to learn and be better.

Personal stories, family, trips, work and personal aspirations were authentic conversation topics that motivated the learners to open up and practice

English. By getting to know and understand each other better, the space for learning became more open and safer. Mauricio's instructor reported that:

> During the conversation part of the evening, we talked a little about the upcoming fourth of July. He said he might go watch fireworks, but he wasn't sure because he needs to rest on some weekends. He commented that fireworks could catch the 'scenery' on fire. In this moment, I saw Mauricio immediately apply his learning into this language. We laughed together at this comment. He wanted to know if I was going to buy any fireworks. I told him a story about when a firecracker went off in my hand when I was little, which he enjoyed. This conversation facilitated more community building. We also talked a bit about the flooding of the local river. Mauricio had helped a friend whose home had been flooded to clean the mud out of his house.

Here, the instructor illustrated how teacher and learner can connect through talking about what is going on in the community and their personal lives. The instructor played a crucial role to keep the students motivated to study and continue to develop their language skills.

The instructor also planned for individual learning activities related to reading and specific grammatical points as requested by the learners. For example, Mauricio and his instructor worked on opposite words and antonyms the second week of class; then they worked on homonyms, homophones and homographs during the third-class meeting:

> Our literacy activity for the evening was to complete worksheet about opposites; Early–Late, Bright–Dark, Tall–Short, etc. One of the questions was the opposite of 'nice'. The answer was 'mean', but Mauricio was puzzled because he was operating from a different definition of the word 'mean'. He asked how it was different than the idea of 'what do you mean?' It took a while to explain the difference. I ended up explaining it in terms of his youngest son – if his son was in trouble, and Mauricio sent him to his room, his son might say, 'My Daddy is mean'. Mauricio understood that explanation. I found it interesting that when I connected it to a familial situation, which is clearly very important and familiar to him, he comprehended more quickly. We returned to the worksheet, exploring the opposites of 'open' and 'closed'. Here was another homonym. Mauricio was operating from the understanding of 'close' as distance such as 'close and far'. I pointed at the door and gave the example of 'the door is closed'. Once I had given him a concrete example, he got it right away.

> It became clear the more I could provide concrete context, the easier he could grasp the concepts. Mauricio said that it makes him happy when he understands what he is learning. Through the discussions that emerged in the learning during this interview, I decided that the next week we would spend some time working with homonyms since those seemed to be particularly difficult for him.

In this interaction, both learner and instructor are learning together. Mauricio is learning new words and new ways to relate to vocabulary words in English, and his instructor is learning about the importance of reflecting on his teaching practice. The instructor is behaving as a participant observer and a reflective instructor. Mauricio's instructor noted that:

> What I thought would require a complex explanation ended up being easier than I thought. For example, the difference between 'sale' and 'sail'. Mauricio understood the word 'sale' to mean when you can purchase items at a discount but was unfamiliar with 'sail'. I simply drew a picture of a boat with a sail for him and he understood.
>
> Because of an explanation about the difference between 'flower' and 'flour', we discussed food. Mauricio asked me if I liked flour tortillas or corn tortillas because he likes both. He noted that food is different at home than Mexican food here in the U.S. His favorite food in Texas is barbecue: brisket, sausage, and mashed potatoes. This was a fun conversation, allowing us to continue building trust.

The instructor used worksheets to provide guidance and structure to his teaching and to focus the second portion of the lesson. The ESL learners used their own tools as well (e.g. smartphones, translation devices, dictionaries, and notebooks).

During the last day of class, we all enjoyed cake and punch together as a celebration for our final evening together. All of us took advantage of this informal gathering to continue to have conversations about what mattered the most to the ESL learners. Mauricio's instructor reported the following:

> During our conversation eating cake, I asked Mauricio more about his job. He shared that he is currently in training to be a foreman at his construction company. He now must learn all the safety regulations and recently had to attend a two-hour meeting. I asked him if it was difficult to understand what the supervisors were saying, and he said that it was and that being able to translate what they say is very important. He explained that mistakes in construction can cost a lot of money and that he wants to get it right.

Half an hour later, learners and instructors adjourned back to the individual work areas for a last session of practice. Mauricio's instructor also reported that:

> Mauricio shared he will soon be going back to the local high school ESL program to continue working on his English literacy skills, yet another example of his commitment and dedication to fulfil his language proficiency goals.

As illustrated above, Mauricio's enthusiasm to learn the language came from both his self-motivation and the instructor's work to motivate him to continue learning. His desire to obtain a GED and create a better future at work are the instrumental motivations and driving forces for L2 learning. Personal stories and work-related topics in construction were exciting topics for Mauricio to discuss. Task motivation and the learner's strategies to study L2 were relevant in Mauricio's case.

Conclusion

The ESL learners had the right attitude to continuing learning English. They were optimistic that they could achieve their goals, and they believed that attending ESL classes would help them achieve their goals learning L2 and more. For example, Viviana reported that:

> When I first came to the United States, I wanted to learn English to be independent, to earn my money, not be afraid, and to change my future. Now, I still come to practice English whenever I can. I want to improve my pronunciation and conversation ability.

Viviana has been studying English on and off for the past 40 years, which illustrates her commitment and effort to learn the language. The motivation to learn English comes from her determination to become a better version of herself as an L2 conversationalist.

> My goal and intent is to formally learn, practice, and become more proficient at English. I am a pastor; I want to offer two church services, one in Spanish and one in English. I need confidence. I need to feel fluent. I need to express all ideas in English. (Esperanza)

Esperanza was aware of the need to reach two different populations through her role as a pastor. Her motivation to improve her conversational English came from her desire to communicate in L2 with her non-Spanish speaking audience. Being a pastor and a spiritual guide for others was part of her professional identity and becoming fluent in English would add to her confidence to do her job. It would help her attain her ideal L2 self.

> I am attending the conversation hour for my daughter. We live close. I help with the children. I take my grandchildren to school and take care them when they need me. I also attend the conversation hour to make friends. I don't have American friends. (Mariela)

Mariela's motivation in learning English related to her family, to building friendship with the locals and workplace expectations. The social and familial aspects of her motivation to learn are strong forces and constitute her determination to improve her performance in L2.

> My motivation to continue learning in ESL is the big desire for improve my life in the USA and communicate fluently in English. Every day when I learn a new word or when I can talk a little bit better with the people is a big motivation for me … My son motivates me … The instructors motivate me in class. (Raul).

Raul explicitly talks about his desire and effort to learn English. He is able to acknowledge that motivation to learn comes from himself and his language instructors.

> My goal to learn English is difficult but no impossible! Learn more for the GED. I have been studying English for two semesters but 5 years living in USA. I need more learn English for my life and job, for my family and the future, to get a better job! When my son tell me 'daddy help me with my homework' I try to help. But it's hard when you don't understand. At work, my boss tell me what to do and I no understand because he speak to fast; he repeat to me slow and ... I understand! (Mauricio).

Mauricio mentioned several reasons why he wanted to learn English: to obtain his GED, to get a better job and for his family and future.

All of the students expressed having a positive attitude about work, life and even difficulties that may emerge from time to time. All of them exhibited desire, effort and the right attitude to learning English. They were motivated by the love for their families, the need to communicate with their children, their ambition to do better at work and to have a better future. They all wanted to improve their living conditions in the USA. They felt the urgency to communicate in English in the workplace and the communities where they lived; they wanted to use what they had learned immediately after class. They all recognized the importance of becoming fluent English users to succeed in achieving their professional and personal goals. They were motivated to learn ESL through desire, effort and positive attitude. Instrumental and integrative motivations fuelled their desire to learn the language. They wanted to learn English to communicate with community members and were moved by integrative motivation to create a sense of belonging and adaptation. Their immigration stories, their desire to achieve their ideal L2-selves and their unique journeys learning L2 propelled them to continue learning.

Recommendations for Practice

(1) Ask students directly what motivates them to continue learning the language.
(2) Share personal stories to encourage the learners to share theirs.
(3) Use photo elicitation (request your students to collect photographs about a topic or focus) and use storytelling to promote oral practice.
(4) Plan conversation activities that allow the learners to discover the areas where they need to improve their English skills.
(5) Reflect on how you as an instructor can promote learner motivation to engage them in L2 learning.

Discussion Questions (Group Activity)

(1) What do instructors learn from listening to the learners' immigration stories?
(2) What can instructors do to get to know their students' learning motivations?
(3) Why is it important to identify learners' L2 motivations?
(4) How can instructors use this knowledge to plan the lessons?
(5) What can instructors do to increase learners' intrinsic motivation?

Part 2
Teachers' Voices

6 ESL Instruction Through Religious Organizations

Religious Organizations Serving Immigrants

Religious organizations have a long history of integrating faith and social services for immigrants. Since the early 1950s religious agencies have sponsored a substantial number of refugees in the United States. In Texas and across the nation, religious organizations offer a wide range of adult education opportunities for all types of immigrants (i.e. refugees, asylees and documented and undocumented immigrants). In addition, church-based ESL programs serve as social mediators, situating immigrants within US communities, empowering their families' literacies, accessing communities of power and having a voice in the larger society (Chao & Mantero, 2014: 108–109). Utilizing narratives provided by Janet, Sarah and Mary, this chapter describes two ESL/literacy programs offered through religious organizations to immigrants. Janet is an Instructor and Director of an ESL program for adults housed in a Catholic church. Mary is the Education Coordinator of a refugee program and Sarah is an ESL instructor for refugees at the same religious organization. Data for this chapter were collected through interviews and conversations at different cafés as well as observations conducted during my visits to these programs.

Church-based ESL and literacy programs are not always federally funded: 'Some churches provide English language services even though they may not qualify for and are not interested in receiving state or federal funding for their programs' (Chao & Kuntz, 2013: 467). Janet's ESL program continues to evolve and improve. Under her direction, the teachers are becoming aware of the need for professional development. The program is funded through community donors and the director is not ready to apply for federal funding. Mary's program is federally funded and serves both refugees and asylees. The teachers in her program have credentials in education and are paid employees.

The first section of the chapter focuses on Janet's narrative about an ESL program housed in a Catholic church. Next, Mary describes her program and the services provided to refugees. Then Sarah describes her experience as an ESL instructor for refugees at the same religious organization where Mary is the program coordinator. The participants' stories are presented in first-person narratives to be as faithful as possible to the experiences shared by these three adult educators.

Janet's ESL program

Janet is in her early 60s and is semi-retired. Her efforts to make the adult ESL program work are driven by her love of the community where she has lived for most of her adult life. Her program is run by volunteer instructors and is funded through community donors.

> Our Catholic Church has had ESL for 7 years. The lady who had it before me, the priest came to her and asked her to do it. When I came on, I taught with her for 3 years, but the program was only open to the people from the church. I said, 'That's not right! You've gotta open it up to the city. Get everybody involved. That's what we want!' So, we finally opened it up two years ago and now we invite all adults in town to come and attend ESL classes. I took over the program two years ago and we have done good. You have to be very flexible with people and their schedules, families, their work, with everything. We try to do that. So, that's helped us. And getting the word out. I'd put out pamphlets anywhere and everywhere I could think of. Taking them to the community center, the different organizations in town, the Housing Authority; taking them to the vegetable stands, taking them to the restaurants. And the program keeps growing and growing.

An important point Janet makes is that sometimes when ESL programs are offered through a religious institution, they only serve those who attend that particular church or share the same religious beliefs. However, she has been successful in opening the program for all to participate in receiving ESL instruction. Another significant aspect of the work that Janet does as program director is getting the word out and recruiting students for the program. Owing to her personal investment in recruiting for the program, they are now running out of space and have a shortage of instructors. They currently operate in the annex to the church which only has four small classrooms and a large meeting room for events. Janet explained that:

> This year, one instructor is going to the public library to teach a class. They have a couple of rooms available there. Although, their rooms stay full, too … and I've tried doing that in the past, and it was full. We definitely have a space problem. We're growing and we need more space. We need more classrooms. I would like to have 12 students per classroom instead of 24; so, that we've got two levels of everything. Of course, that's going to mean more teachers which is also an issue. And I'd like to get the school district involved with this. I think they need to be.

Janet's program needs to find a more permanent solution to the problem of space and lack of instructors. The space where classes are held is not adequate for teaching. The four classrooms are small, have poor lighting and do not have appropriate furniture for holding a class. She is well aware of these issues and is currently looking for a solution.

> There might be a solution but that would mean getting federal funding and so ... the bureaucracy begins! Have you ever seen what the students have to complete as enrolment to come to these classes? It's almost like a book ... to obtain the federal funding. We have enough trouble as is to keep them coming to class to also start asking so many questions about their personal lives. Crazy! Program directors also have tons of reporting to do. They would start telling us what to do and how to teach our classes. There will be no freedom.

The easiest solution for the problem of space, lack of instructors and resources would be for Janet's program to join the state literacy agency. However, she is aware that, with obtaining the funding, other issues, such as accountability measures and implementation of adult ESL standards, will also follow. As she explains, her best option to continue to enjoy the freedom that the current program offers would be to join forces with the local school district.

> I've been thinking hard, and the place I'd rather partner with the most is the district. I think that would be really significant if I could get space to teach the ESL classes over at the school district. And that's why I was really happy in August. You know that guy who was there the opening night back in August? He's the new bilingual coordinator for the district. I want to ask him for help for next year.

> Last night at the school board debate, people were saying that our school district here is not good. And it's not going to get better until we start educating our parents more and teaching them. I think this is the right motivation to get the parents involved in learning English. They need to be able to go to the school and learn about what their kids are doing. They're a great example to their own children by coming and wanting to learn a new language and coming to school. I'm really trying to promote that.

Another challenge Janet is facing is student attrition; she actively recruits for the program, and each year they start with a large enrolment that gets reduced to 50% by the end of the school year. The program goes from August to May to mimic the public-school calendar system.

> Now we have about 60+ students; we had 40+ last year. But we ended up with only 25 at the end of the year. I'm watching that very carefully this year. Last year, our biggest drop was in ESL level 1, where we lost a whole bunch of students, and that's why I was going to go get some of the higher-level students to come down to give testimonials to say, 'I was here. I know that you can do it!' I am inviting this student who's been in the program for 5 years. He has zero education. Zero. He never went to

school. He was born in Mexico, worked in the fields. He wants to own his own business as a framer. He's actually a framer's boss. Does he speak well? Does he have a hard time writing? But he's gone up to a level 3. He's good. He's getting better. He's an inspiration. And he comes to class, except I'm worried. He used to come to class, never missed a class, always there, and he now has missed 3 lessons in a row. I have texted him, but now I need to call him to see what's going on. He was getting ready to go to level 4!

It is important to acknowledge that the ESL teachers in this program are volunteers who come from different careers. Only one of them is an ESL teacher at a high school and another has a master's in Adult Education. Janet's background is in real estate. Because their program is not affiliated with any of the state literacy organizations, they are not required to receive the mandatory annual 12 hours of professional development that federally funded programs require. However, they attend professional development focusing on ESL teaching when time and resources allow. They teach in the program because it is a way to give back to the community. Thus, their professionalism is defined not just by having a degree in TESOL but also by having a 'professional standing in the following areas: classroom management, motivation to participate in professional development, appropriate attire used by teachers, and understanding the needs of adult learners' (Brown & Bywater, 2009/2010: 2005). Accordingly, Janet tries to discuss students' issues and teaching tips at the faculty meetings:

> We meet once or twice a semester for a faculty meeting and discuss program issues. This past meeting, we talked about how to correct students when they make mistakes. I tell them at the start of class we make mistakes. I want you to make mistakes. I make mistakes. Correct me. It's just that ... that's why we're here. If you aren't making mistakes, you already know it. So, some guy just said [L] the other day. I said, what did you say? He said [L]. Say it again. Say it again. And he laughs. And everybody laughed. It becomes a fun thing. It's more of a light take on life. It's gonna help them. I tell them, you can know all the English you want, and you can read it and write it, but if people don't understand you? So, you've got to be understood!

The faculty meetings at Janet's program may not be enough time for the instructors to discuss program issues and obtain professional development. Ongoing professional development should include the 'study of the English language, theories of second language acquisition, adult learners and the social context in which they live and work, and teaching methodology and materials development that reflect the realities of the students' lives' (Orem, 2005: 111). Professional development for the teachers is an area for improvement that as a program director Janet is aware of as well as the need to continue monitoring why students drop off the program in large numbers from the first two ESL levels. Thus, she reported the following:

> My strongest teachers have to be in levels 1 and 2. Our strongest now is Lucy in level 1, we're teaching phonics. Because I do think that's important because at level 3, nobody knows how to pronounce [th] or the difference between [sh] and [ch]. Yes, we get students at level 2 and 3 who bypassed level 1 because of their expertise on the assessment test. At least we're getting some of that started. In level 1, we have one strong teacher. Unfortunately, levels 1 and 2 have two teachers each, two teachers come on Monday and two different ones come on Thursday. I know it is a problem, but it's the best I can do for now. This is volunteer work and those teachers were not able to commit to come both days. So, each of them teaches once a week.

Having students not returning to class in community-based programs is not surprising but having 50% student attrition is a reason for concern. A piece of advice for Janet would be to rotate the instructors so they do not teach the same ESL student level all of the time. This may motivate them to prepare the lessons for a new course level. Also, the most experienced and better qualified instructors should be appointed to ESL levels 1 and 2 in hope that it makes a difference in student retention, but she needs to have instructors that can make it to class both days. Currently, they do not have an established program curriculum and use a commercial textbook, which they follow page by page in each lesson. Having a textbook is good for guiding the instructors, but they should also be aware that the textbook provides *the what*, the content, and it is the role of the instructor to know *the how*, the pedagogy. How they deliver the content from the textbook is equally important for student success. Teachers' self-confidence as grounded in professional competence (Freire, 2001) remains an issue to be addressed here. The teachers need to know how to teach and not just follow a textbook page by page.

Mary's refugee program

Mary is in her early 40s and is the Education Coordinator for a refugee program in Central Texas. In her own words, the purpose of the program is 'to provide refugees with services they need like housing, employment, education and acculturation, and to help them achieve self-sufficiency as quickly as possible'. Mary continues to explain that:

> We are notified in advance of who will join the program. We make the arrangements before they come, we wait for them at the airport, we help them with the documentation process. We also prepare meals for them and whatever supplies they need for arrival. On the next day, we enrol them in a lot of services like education courses, ESL included, training and employment, and acculturation assistance. However, housing services and the food stamps program are provided only up to 6 months.

> As the first step to help refugees to be able to have job opportunities, we make sure to improve their language skills by providing ESL classes as well as acculturation assistance to develop independence and self-sufficiency. Language and acculturation education is offered up to 5 years. For example, if a refugee needs to have electricity services, they attend a program to introduce them to the process and steps necessary to obtain this service. Also, a refugee who has been classified to attend ESL classes should enrol in at least 80 hours of instruction. After that, the program coordinator post-tests them to measure ESL learning for completion of the program and to justify the funding we receive.

For most new arrivals, not just refugees, obtaining services to resettle in the new country (e.g. housing, employment, transportation and children's schooling) can become a daunting task. These are important topics for discussion in the ESL classroom. The instructor can dedicate a portion of the class time to answering questions and providing information that the students need to be able to access public services. Next, Mary continues to explain other services offered to refugees in her program:

> We offer family literacy, which consist of three different classes: literacy for parents, literacy for children, and literacy for parent and child integration. Parents and children practice literacy and apply the information they have learned during the day. For instance, the parent would be educated about a health issue, the child would learn about spelling and the parts of the body. By the end of the day, both meet in class to practice the integration of the knowledge they acquired. We make sure that they enrol in the Medicaid Plan and that parents understand their responsibility towards family health.
>
> We have more than 60 family and community experts who provide strategies and plans to assist refugees to obtain self-sufficiency. We also provide several workshops to bridge the gap among parents, children, and schools. These initiatives are part of the family literacy programs and the acculturation assistance.

Brown and Bywater (2009/2010) argue that current adult education does not focus just on the Americanization of students; adult education programs 'seek not only to teach students about American culture and the language used, but also to prepare them to live as self-reliant individuals' (2009/2010: 203). Similarly, adults participating in refugee programs are expected to become self-sufficient and provide for their families within six months of arrival. Mary's program is aware of the need to continue to provide education services and acculturation support even after this deadline is accomplished. She describes other family literacy initiatives helping to achieve this goal – learners reaching self-sufficiency to provide for their families:

An additional program is 'family gardening' as part of the acculturation assistance. Through this program, a person can share their cultural traditions. This program supports family literacy development as two or three generations get involved. Besides the local plants, the families are inspired to grow vegetables, plants and herbs from their backgrounds. They bring recipes and share meals whenever possible.

Here, Mary illustrates one of the reciprocal social benefits of participating in the community garden. In particular, a study by Hartwig and Mason (2016: 1157) on refugee gardeners reported on the social benefits, including: enjoying gardening with family and friends, helping and giving each other advice on when to plant, water and harvest, and interacting with friends and neighbors who simply want to take a look at the garden plots, enjoy time outside and interact with people in the neighborhood or church members.

Sarah's experience teaching refugees

Sarah is in her early 30s and taught English abroad and in the USA for eight years before starting to teach in the refugee program. She worked for three years in this program then accepted a full-time position as the Coordinator of Adult Education Programs at a different organization. What is remarkable about her story is the fact that even experienced teachers need to continue learning and get to know the setting and conditions of their students to teach ESL lessons that are relevant to students. Sarah shared in her interview that:

> We did not receive any training to teach at the refugee program; we were just assigned a group. Luckily, I was in graduate school doing a master's in Adult Education and majoring in ESL at the time. I immediately started to apply what I was learning to my teaching. I took my graduate class projects, and I molded them into learning about what I was doing. For example, refugee policy which was really important, and I noticed that my co-workers had no idea. All this information is publicly available of course. But you have to study to learn it; you have to make the time. I learned about it and wrote about it for my classes. My co-workers had no idea about the way the money was flowing and the reason why we were receiving this grant or another. But yeah, in the program, we got paid close to nothing. I got paid $12 an hour, you know, and no training.

Similar to what happens in other programs, Sarah and her co-workers did not receive training on program expectations or adequate pedagogy training to teach these particular learners. Often, the assumption is that the instructor will learn from on-the-job training and make the time to

72 Part 2: Teachers' Voices

Figure 6.1 Community garden image provided by Sarah

learn from others and from the students to become effective in the program.

> A memorable experience was when we started a refugee community garden [see Figure 6.1]. I started it, it was an abandoned space with just tall grass growing. I got $5,000 for a start-up grant for community gardens. I started teaching in there. And at the time, I was working with the Karenni refugees who were kind of agrarian folks who have a very large learning curve. For example, learning how to fill out a form, even if it's translated, it took them a long time to learn how to do it. They have an oral language tradition, and everything's totally different in writing, you know. They also bring their babies to class; they're nursing during class. Babies are peeing. They don't wear diapers. Then, to learn something like filling out a form might take a while, and it is not as pressing as taking care of family. So, it's difficult to have all these expectations that they will learn and behave as traditional students.

In explaining how the community garden got started, Sarah goes on a tangent to describe the characteristics of the students she had at that time. It is important to highlight this in her narrative because the community garden was the medium that allowed her to address some of the difficulties she was facing while trying to teach these students. The community garden allowed her to authentically engage her Karenni students in learning and practicing English.

> When we first started the community garden, it was barely even dug out, but I started having the class outside and without any kind of paper. I was trying to implement the oral tradition style Karenni students identified with the most. And it was immediately like their eyes were open and bright. They wanted to get engaged; they wanted to do

it all. They brought children and friends along. This space became therapeutical to them; it became a meeting place and lots of incidental learning took place. I tried to be there as much as I could, and English was always flowing. They learned about local plants and taught each other about the plants and herbs from their cultures. They also shared anecdotes from their countries and their experiences with agriculture. This was a space of joy where I could teach, and they could learn about relevant stuff.

In her narrative, Sarah reports on how the instructor in a refugee program needs to become a linguistic, cultural and community bridge. Her assertions correlate with the findings in a study conducted by Hartwig and Mason (2016) focusing on Karen and Bhutanese populations. They discovered how gardens are a meaningful health promotion intervention for refugees and immigrants adjusting to the complexity of their new lives in the USA and coping with past traumas. In Sarah's case, the instructor and the students found multiple benefits from participating in the community garden. The adults became engaged in learning, shared knowledge and told stories to teach about plants and herbs.

Given the large population of refugees coming to live in the United States, Mary and Sarah's narratives are relevant today. As a matter of fact, the Pew Research Center (2016) reports that in 2015, 70,000 refugees entered the country. In 2016, 85,000 refugees were accepted in the United States.

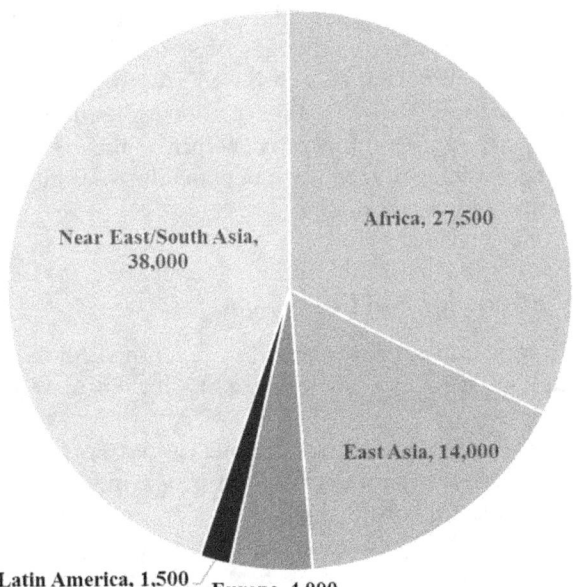

Figure 6.2 Refugee arrivals to the USA, 2016

As illustrated in Figure 6.2, the number of refugees accepted in the United States increased by 15,000. The largest number of refugees in 2016 came from Near East/South Asia. This figure is a product of the political and war conflict in Syria and other neighboring countries. Likewise, data extracted from the Worldwide Refugee Admissions Processing System on 16 September 2016 illustrate refugee arrivals by placement state. The top seven states where refugees were relocated included: Texas (1779), California (1380), Michigan (958), Washington (501), Arizona (421), Illinois (412) and New York (406). Thus, Texas receives a large number of refugees, making Mary and Sarah's narratives very relevant.

Conclusion

The contributions of religious organizations offering ESL instruction are many. Research suggests that participation in church-sponsored ESL programs empowers family literacy and the use of home language (Chao & Mantero, 2014). These programs are essential to community development and to assisting immigrants to acculturate and incorporate to US society and the workforce. Data from the *National Population Projection* report show that 42.4 million immigrants (documented and undocumented) now live in the country and at least 45% are in need of ESL instruction (United States Census Bureau, 2014). However, there are not enough publicly funded programs to serve all immigrants in need of learning ESL.

Establishing partnerships and collaborations among institutions in the community can address the challenges of space, funding and need for professional development that church-based programs face. For example, partnering with school districts for space allocation and with universities for professional development may prove helpful. Likewise, family literacy and community garden programs are beneficial for language acquisition and acculturation of immigrants.

Recommendations for Practice

(1) Promote family literacy practices while teaching ESL to adults. Adults learn language through socializing in authentic family learning situations.
(2) Create collaborations with local organizations to provide the different services needed by the students in your program.
(3) Subscribe to TESOL professional listservs, and participate in webinars and other online free resources for ESL teachers.
(4) Be proactive about your own professional development and engagement in research.

Discussion Questions (Group Activity)

(1) What are some creative suggestions for church-sponsored programs to provide adequate professional development for their instructors?
(2) What should instructors know about curriculum instruction to teach ESL to refugees and immigrants?
(3) What do you know about refugee programs and the education services they offer?
(4) How is it different to teach ESL and literacy to refugees compared with other types of immigrants?

7 Public Libraries Building Literate Communities

Public Libraries Building Literate Communities

The role of the public library in helping adult immigrants to further develop ESL proficiency is of critical importance. From the start, public libraries were charged with supporting adult education and learning. However, for a while they were seen as repositories of books and information. During recent decades, their role has evolved to become promoters of community development, helping adults to improve the quality of their lives (Shrestha & Krolak, 2015). Thus, public libraries have become community development centers focusing on social empowerment, economic development and lifelong learning (Shrestha & Krolak, 2015). After War World II libraries started to be recognized as having the potential to develop literate citizens by teaching literacy, job skills and cultural knowledge (Peich & Fletcher, 2015).

Public libraries support all of the realms of life-wide learning: formal education, workforce development, literacy development, quality-of-life issues and informal learning for all types of citizens (Norman, 2012: 95). As early as the 1920s, public libraries played an important role in the development of literacy skills for new Americans to succeed in the new country as well as providing learning opportunities for those without access to formal education (Peich & Fletcher, 2015). Concerning literacy, the American Library Association supports libraries with the task of helping children and adults to develop reading and computer literacy with the understanding that the ability to seek and effectively utilize information resources is essential in a global information society (American Library Association, 2010: 3). Therefore, this chapter documents the experiences of Daisy working as a Librarian and Coordinator of Adult Education Programs at a medium-sized public library in Central Texas.

Daisy's Experiences as Librarian and Coordinator

Daisy is in her mid-30s and holds two master's degrees, one in Adult Education and the other in Library Science. She has been at her current position serving as Coordinator of Adult Education Programs for the past two years. Before working at the library, she was an instructor of ESL and GED for 10 years. In the following pages she describes the role of the public library, the different programs for adults they offer and the challenges she faces identifying community needs to offer relevant adult education programs. From the interviews conducted with Daisy, it became evident that, for her, *adult education* means assisting adults to acquire skills that will help them function and participate in society not only in the workplace but also in everyday life and relationships. Daisy reported that:

> An adult learner is just anybody who had the time and transportation and will to come to the library. It's diverse, but I worry about the folks that aren't coming to the library. I wonder if maybe some people could get a lot of use out of the library but aren't coming to the library at all. I always wonder what could be done to make the library services more accessible and how to attract those patrons who are not coming. At the library, we offer adult basic education in the form of ESL classes, GED, and financial literacy, all in collaboration with experts in the community. We also offer health and wellness related programs such as nutrition and suicide prevention. But one difficulty I have is figuring out the needs of the community. There's not a needs assessment tool that I can use. It's a moving target. Right now, I just guess what could be useful to the community. I also look at program attendance and that gives me a clue as to what people are liking. We don't collect their names and information when they attend an event; we just do a headcount.

The library is a department of the city; the budget they receive is not stipulated by how many people come to their programs, what they learn or their goals like what happens to those associated with adult education and literacy organizations. It would be useful if they did a survey in the community to identify their learning needs. For now, Daisy relies on local experts and opportunities for programs to become available, so she can utilize them. She states that:

> Usually, programs come to my door. University professors want to come and do a workshop or teach a class as a way to connect with community. Other times, experts come to me wanting to offer a program or share a specific skill. The example of a program that I had to do outreach to find somebody who was certified and could do such program was the suicide prevention program. I make sure that whatever program we offer is a quality program and is offered by qualified people. For example, I also invited a specialist in parent education to offer a workshop for parents on how to discipline their children, how to communicate with them, and how to help them have a dialogue.

Daisy makes a good point here; community education needs to be quality education regardless of the topic or the target audience. Public libraries are open to all people and provide services that benefit individuals from all ages and from all cultural backgrounds. Other important services provided at her library relate to assisting ESL learners with resume writing, computer classes and ESL classes. At this public library, their space is limited, and they currently offer only two classes of ESL one of which Daisy teaches.

My partnership with this library has been by offering three programs, one for ESL conversation for adults, another for numeracy instruction for parents and a program on health literacy instruction for families. During the summer time, when most adult ESL programs are on vacation, the students from the graduate program where I work come with me to volunteer as conversation partners with adults learning ESL.

> Space is an issue at times. We have two classrooms, but they are usually booked. I just reserved Wednesdays to teach an ESL class for a group of students who were on a waiting list to get in classes with the ESL program offered at a local church, around ten people. I got some left-over textbooks from when I was teaching ESL two years ago, and that is what I will be using for this class. My plan was to reach out to you to see if you had a graduate student, an intern, wanting to learn how to teach to assist me and maybe substitute for me on the evenings when I am not here.

The city and the community learning needs have grown, but the space at the public library continues to be the same. Likewise, volunteers with appropriate qualifications to teach ESL are on demand. Daisy cannot do everything and, as a full-time employee of the library, her schedule requires her to be there early in the morning. Teaching at night is not always possible for her owing to family responsibilities. However, she continues to look for solutions, is inquisitive and has some advice to share with the local governmental agencies.

Educating the whole person

Daisy understands the need for adult learners to become more marketable when obtaining a GED or achieving ESL proficiency for the workplace. However, she believes it is only one aspect of what adult education should be doing. In her interview she shared the following:

> I recently wrote a grant that was approved, and we already used the funds. It all happened in a matter of weeks, but the grant was from an interesting collaboration between The Texas Workforce Commission (TWC) and Texas Libraries and Archives Commission. If I worked for Workforce, I would give it back to the Texas Education Agency (TEA). Three years ago, TEA was administering adult education programs, they weren't perfect, but they were doing better. Looking at the mind shift that happened ... We went from thinking about people as human beings with learning needs to thinking of them as workers. The current curriculum requirements are sometimes ridiculous. For example, you're teaching ... say, a family literacy class, you're teaching ESL to moms while their children are doing another lesson. Well now, because your grant is under

Workforce, you have to incorporate elements of how they can get a job or improve in their job and these are stay at home moms. It makes no sense. TEA understood people needed to participate in different programs and for different purposes. Not everybody is looking for a job or can get a job; some of our patrons are stay-at-home moms or dads.

Daisy's assertions agree with current literature on the vital role of the libraries in educating patrons to cover different aspects of their lives as adults. As Peich and Fletcher (2015) remind us: 'Contemporary public libraries have proven valuable at providing lifelong learning in response to rapidly changing developments in technology, volatile economies, and shifting demographics' (2015: 50). The resources and programs offered by public libraries should support a variety of lifelong learning opportunities for adults. In Daisy's words:

> Preparing adults for the workforce is a really important aspect of both ESL and GED, but it's just one aspect. Understanding how to become a good citizen is another important piece, like how to improve your health and communicate with your doctor, how to use technology, how to get insurance, how to get your children enrolled in school … there's more to educating adults than just helping them qualify for a job! There's so much more to being a human being than just being a worker!

Daisy has a strong opinion, and she relies on her prior experiences working as an adult ESL and GED instructor at different programs. This population of students has a variety of needs that are equally important as obtaining a job. Learning to navigate the different systems (e.g. transportation, health, housing, school) in the new country is a complex task for immigrants.

Nuances of both the resettlement and acculturation processes should be addressed in ESL and GED instruction. As stated by Chapman *et al.* (2006), lifelong learning embraces three overarching principles: 'learning for a more highly skilled workforce and strong economy, learning for a better democracy and an inclusive society, and learning for a more personally rewarding life' (2006: 152). Unfortunately, politicians and new policies seem to disregard the education of immigrants and low-income citizens when it comes to addressing these three principles. Becoming involved in the practice of democracy and learning for enjoyment get relegated and seem irrelevant.

Fear of becoming obsolete

In the following section Daisy addresses two issues: (1) librarians' fear of libraries becoming obsolete; and (2) the fact that ESL/literacy teaching is an important job, but it has low remuneration. She reflects on the need for state agencies to allocate funding for offering ESL teachers a better remuneration for their services. She also explains how libraries are at risk if they do not keep up with technological advances.

> TWC should assign a portion of their budget to paying ESL teachers of adults. When they are well paid, they make $20 an hour, yes, they work two-hour classes three days a week and they get one-hour preparation, but who can live on that salary? They don't get any insurance or benefits; it's always a part-time job. You have to get at least three jobs just to pay rent and eat. That's the life of an adult education teacher. It's not fantastic! Now TWC is not even putting money into that, a pitiful bucket which is getting more pitiful and the rationale is … 'Well, it would be cheaper for adults to learn in places like public libraries because library staff already has jobs … '. I think it's our fault, too because we have a fear of being thought of as not needed or obsolete because of Google and e-books and technology. We want people to know that we are *digital literacy centers*. We are a hub of all kinds of resources, including a person to guide you through resources, navigate loads of information and even help you figure out what's fake and what's real. Bottom line is, we don't want to lose our jobs!

Daisy has an interesting view of what is happening to libraries and the impact of recent policies. In the neighboring city where she used to work, libraries are changing in a big way, and she is afraid that is a political trend.

> We are supposed to be centers of adult education. That's the whole idea! As I mentioned before, in the city next door, seven adult education buildings, beautiful structures, built for adult education were closed. In this city, there is at least a 25% illiteracy. I'm talking about functional literacy and 25% is quite high. As I was saying, the buildings were just ten years old and with interesting architecture, with excellent classroom space, a nice lobby area and staffed with lots of levels of ESL and GED classes. They were even offering other classes, German, Zumba, and yoga. These were really excellent places! This was probably the doing of a former mayor, by the way … However, by shutting down these seven literacy adult education buildings and reallocating the money into library projects, they saved tons of money or that's what they think!

No matter how good a library is at providing education opportunities for individuals in the community, they are already working above their capacity offering their own programs, and they do not have enough staff and instructors to also offer ESL and GED instruction on a regular basis. Daisy is right in criticizing this decision made by local politicians. The savings they think are happening will accumulate as debt once the desired results of creating literate communities does not happen at the same rate and pace as it used to happen.

In the next section Daisy explains about her efforts to help the library keep current by purchasing Mondopads, a software to assist GED students lean and practice using technology:

> When I was hired, my budget was extraordinary! It was huge compared to what I knew from working in the field of adult education where I used

to do everything for free. Every single program was free for the students. I never bought anything to teach because the salary I received would not allow for me to afford buying class materials out of pocket. I was very resourceful and there are so many authentic materials out there that are free ... I used to go to a pharmacy or the supermarket and grab the grocery pamphlet for example. I could teach class just using that. It's colorful, real, familiar, and free!

Even though Daisy is currently a librarian, her prior experiences teaching ESL and GED for publicly funded programs are relevant to be able to understand the decisions she has made as Coordinator of Adult Education Programs at the library. Daisy continues to tell about how technology alone may not be useful in helping prepare GED learners.

As I was saying, I had this budget that was so huge, and I felt excited to have that power because, as an ESL teacher, I just never had a budget. This was a huge budget, and I love libraries. But looking back, after I spent it all, I mean, I bought these Mondopads, a software to practice for GED [see Figure 7.1]. Because in nonprofit world when you have a grant, and you're at the end of the fiscal year you've got to use it or lose it! If you don't use it, they're going to think that you don't need it.

Now that we had computers and software, we were supposed to put GED students on the computer. They would log in, register with emails, learn and practice independently. Truth is, it was a total fiasco!!! If you've ever hung out with GED students, you would know. This was completely mismatched to a lot of people's learning styles. It did not help retention. People didn't stick around. Nobody ever came back. Right now, there's practically no GED programs going on.

In her narrative, Daisy makes the point that having the budget is not everything when designing adult education. She was more successful when

Figure 7.1 Mondopads for the library

using a *low-tech* approach to instruction by utilizing authentic learning materials such as the supermarket pamphlets.

It is important to keep in mind that adults need to be prepared to use technology to be able to learn on their own. Often the learners who enroll in ESL and GED programs are non-traditional students, and they need extra assistance and encouragement to achieve their learning goals. They still need the guidance of an instructor when using technology. Just interacting with computer software is not good enough for some learners. Technology can present a challenge for adults and prevent them from participation in education. For technology to be less challenging for ESL and GED adults, it should require the user to take fewer actions, such as providing different modes of feedback, require the use of simple commands and be intuitive to the user (Patomella *et al.*, 2013).

Library patrons' learning needs

Next, Daisy continues to discuss library patrons' learning needs. She specifically talks about how diverse these learning needs are and the specific learning needs of the immigrant learners who visit the library.

> Well, you know, libraries are traditionally places for immigrants. And so, what happens every day is that I'm on the reference desk and somebody comes up to me and they say, 'I need information about … ' and they tell me what their learning need is. Their needs of adult immigrants are so diverse … overcome technology anxiety, create an email account, print and understand their W2, understand how to file taxes, apply for employment, or build a resume. I give them all available information, call the social service provider, and find out if they can actually provide the service for this person. If they have to go to the actual place, I also give them a map or directions to get to the place. Unfortunately, I can't help all patrons the same way. I try, but I don't always have the time. But I do try to understand the need more, so I can program for a workshop or event to help more than one person at a time.

Daisy presents several important issues here as she comes back to the topic of technology anxiety, the diverse needs of library patrons, in general, and the learning needs of immigrants in particular. Similarly, a study conducted by Armstrong (2015) on ESL and low-income computer literacy learners discusses her work teaching technology to adults in a public library. Armstrong describes the demographics of the patrons she serves as 'immigrant young adults still learning English, older adults, who are mostly native speakers and African American, and other adults pursuing technology education such as online degrees or certifications' (2015: 135). These are similar characteristics to the population served at Daisy's library. Both librarians encountered similar difficulties when trying to implement the principles of self-directed learning with adults using technology to learn by themselves.

To gain a better understanding of this issue, it is important to explain that self-directed learning refers to 'learning in which decisions around what to learn, how to learn it, and how to decide if one has learned something well enough are all in the hands of the learners' (Brookfield, 2013: 90). In addition, there is a four-stage model suggested by Grow (1991) to understand how adults can learn to become self-directed learners. This model suggests a progression from dependent learner to self-directed learner and the respective role of the teacher in each stage. In stage 1 the learners are low in self-direction, and the teacher's role is that of an authority coach. Stage 2 presents the learners with moderate self-direction and the teacher is a motivator and guide. Stage 3 describes the learners as having intermediate self-direction and the teacher as a facilitator. Lastly, stage 4 presents the learners with high self-direction and the teacher as a consultant and delegator.

It seems that, at Daisy's library, they expected the learners to be at stage 4 of the self-directed model proposed by Grow (1991). Likewise, Armstrong (2015) explained that expecting adults to be self-directed learners when learning new technology or learning on their own using technology could be counterproductive:

> On occasion, the goal of some classes simply becomes to reduce technology-related anxiety, ahead even of the official class objectives. In addition to anxiety and lack of self-confidence, the differing cultural backgrounds of my students could also sometimes be a barrier to a movement towards self-direction. (2015: 137)

This is very similar to what happened at Daisy's library trying to have adults practice for the GED exam using the Mondopads that she so enthusiastically purchased for the library. The learners would have to face the software to study for the GED alone, but they did not have an orientation class preparing them to use the software, or to explain the potential benefits of using it. In this case, looking at Grow's (1991) four stages of self-directed learning model may prove beneficial. A recommendation would be to assess the level of self-directedness of the library patrons and group them by stages until they become fully independent using technology to study for the GED.

Daisy also spoke about the diverse needs of library patrons and the specific learning needs of immigrants. Besides the need to overcome technology anxiety, other learning needs for immigrants she identified included 'create an email account, print and understand their W2, understand how to file taxes, apply for employment, and build a resume'. These are cultural concepts that may seem foreign to immigrants coming from diverse nationalities, backgrounds, and traditions. In some cultures, for example, activities such as filing taxes and applying for a job are carried out in collaboration with others by utilizing social and human capital that they still do not possess in the new country. Daisy is aware of this and that is why she is committed to providing support for these library patrons to make sure their needs are met.

Conclusion

This chapter described the public library as a space for promoting the literacy skills of local communities. With adult education policies continually changing and the budget cuts to programs, libraries continue to become more and more important in offering a variety of programs and literacy instruction to adults and families in the local communities. Efforts to serve the community such as the work that Daisy is doing are commendable! However, public librarians also need to have relevant opportunities to participate in professional development so that they make wise decisions about important issues such as how to assess community learning needs, how to design relevant programs to serve adults and families and how to train adults to become self-directed learners.

Public libraries play a crucial role in the education of immigrants and low-income adults. Librarians have the power to determine the overall success of a community library; they are gatekeepers of services and information for adults to have access to further education and learning. Community libraries can promote the creation of literate communities as well as supporting personal and community development for their patrons.

Recommendations for Practice

(1) Find out what the library can offer to your ESL students. Do a fieldtrip to the public library with your students and help them obtain a library card.
(2) Promote and support the use of your local public library.
(3) Inform librarians about your students' learning needs to help them identify learning programs needed in the local community.
(4) Consider providing an orientation session whenever you require ESL and GED students to use technology and new software for learning purposes.
(5) Survey your students' knowledge and perceptions about the use of technology and software to learn on their own.

Discussion Questions (Group Activity)

(1) What is your opinion about public libraries taking over the work of adult learning centers?
(2) How can adult education teachers assist learners to overcome technology-related anxiety so that they can become self-directed learners?
(3) In what teaching scenarios would you implement Grow's (1991) four stages of self-directed learning model?

8 Engaged Scholarship Training TESOL Instructors

Training TESOL Instructors

The narratives shared in this chapter come from actual graduate students gaining training in TESOL. In this chapter, they are referred to as teacher-learners. The rationale behind this word choice is that some of the graduate students have teaching experience prior to enrolling in the master's program, some have just obtained jobs teaching English to adults and others have no experience teaching but aspire to become TESOL instructors. Brody *et al.* (2010) use the term 'professional socialization' to refer to the process of becoming a professional. They further explain that professional socialization is 'the process of developing a role-based identity with values, norms, and symbols that may span many organizations within or across multiple fields. This type of socialization facilitates acquisition of the skills, knowledge, and attitudes necessary to fulfill the duties of this role' (Brody *et al.*, 2010: 615–16). To facilitate the professional socialization of TESOL instructors and use a balanced theory–practice approach, this chapter describes their participation in a variety of interactive learning experiences within the context of the local communities such as conducting classroom observations, tutoring adult English learners, serving as conversation partners for adult English learners and participating in internships. As illustrated through the narratives shared in this chapter, these projects are framed utilizing an engaged scholarship approach to service the local communities.

To capture and analyze their experiences while participating in these learning events, the teacher-learners were required to maintain a journal and reflect in writing on how they envisioned and enacted teaching. Borg (2001: 157) explained that, by documenting and reflecting on their experience by keeping this reflective journal, the teachers benefit by developing an enhanced awareness of themselves as people and professionals, an awareness which makes for more informed professional decision making. While writing the journal entries, the teacher-learners identified a concern, articulated these ideas in writing, analyzed a problem or situation, brought their feelings out into the open, and identified a course of action.

They shared their reflection with other teachers and discussed ways to approach difficult situations and to problem solve. As Freire (2001: 31) stated: 'through the practice of teaching that is also learning and learning that is also teaching, we are participating in a total experience that is simultaneously pedagogical, ethical, and collaborative'. The teacher-learners needed to become attentive observers and active learners to apply the new learning in connection to the theory they were studying. Engaging in critical reflection and sharing their learning with other TESOL instructors were crucial to the practice of engaged scholarship.

Engaged Scholarship

Engaged scholarship entails a reciprocal partnership with the community, is interdisciplinary and integrates teaching, research and service (Boyer, 1990, 1996; Elwell & Bean, 2001). All of the activities described in this chapter were possible thanks to the collaboration of organizations and stakeholders in the local community. They welcomed the teacher-learners in their programs and classrooms to allow them to learn and provide some type of service in return. Engaged scholarship entails the collaboration between academics and individuals outside of the academy for the mutually beneficial exchange of knowledge and resources in a context of partnership and reciprocity (Boyer, 1996; Elwell & Bean, 2001; Lebeau & Bennion, 2014; Udall *et al.*, 2015). At the university, the teacher-learners study theory disconnected from the immediate practice. Elwell and Bean (2001) state: 'By working on a community service project, students apply classroom knowledge to real-world experiences and use real-world experiences to inform classroom knowledge' (2001: 48). Therefore, it makes sense for all higher education courses to include at least one project that forces students to connect and work with the community and the programs where they will work upon graduation.

The scholarship of engagement includes explicitly democratic dimensions of encouraging the participation of non-academics in ways that enhance and broaden engagement and deliberation about major social issues inside and outside the university (Boyer, 1996; Lebeau & Bennion, 2014; Udall *et al.*, 2015). In this case, the social issues that connected practitioners and the teacher-learners related to the need to provide high-quality English teaching, literacy instruction and other forms of education relevant to the adults in the community. Through engaged scholarship, university students gain knowledge and benefit from learning with and from community members such as TESOL-instructors that are more experienced and the adult learners they served. 'Universities frequently frame public engagement projects as "doing good" for partner organizations without explicitly acknowledging the "good" partners contribute to the University' (Udall *et al.*, 2015: 161). Keeping this in mind, within this practice of engaged scholarship and with the goal of contributing to the education of adults in their communities, the teacher-learners reflected about how and from whom they were learning since engaged scholarship is a bidirectional learning activity (Boyer, 1996; Elwell & Bean, 2001; Udall et al., 2015). Accordingly, the teacher-learners participated in different learning events and conducted classroom observations, tutored adult English learners, served as conversation partners and participated in internship practices.

Conducting TESOL classroom observations

> I noticed how difficult it was for learners to keep focused for the class duration which is four hours. All of them come to class after they leave their jobs. Some of them have families and children that they are taking care of. Class starts every day at 5:00 and ends at 9:00, some students come late, and others leave earlier due to transportation issues. The first hour they are all working hard, sharing stories about their workday or sharing stories about their families. During the second hour, learners will continue to work. They will eat their dinner, drink some refreshments and take some breaks. Toward the third hour, signs of exhaustion will appear in most of the students. By the fourth hour, almost everyone is completely drained and incapable of continuing. Sometimes, they will ask to leave early, and others will try until it is the time to leave. I learned from this observation to take into consideration the circumstances of learners especially if evening classes and for working learners. (Amari's journal entry)

Similar to Amari above, the teacher-learners visit adult education centers and adult education organizations to become familiar with these programs, the learners and the teaching practices of instructors working with adult learners. The teacher-learners receive examples of observation protocols and select the one they want to use. Normally these observation protocols include the same list of elements to conduct the classroom observation. The teacher-learners can customize the observation protocol, but they needed to keep in mind their graduate course requirements and the theory-practice connection (see Table 8.1).

Keeping in mind the theory learned in the university classroom, during their observation practice, the teacher-learners take notes and reflect in writing on what to report for these observations. Freire (2001) emphasized, 'Critical reflection on practice is a requirement of the relationship between theory and practice. Otherwise, theory becomes simply "blah, blah, blah", and practice, pure activism' (2001: 30). The teacher-learners use the journal as a tool for reflection and as a source of information and analysis when writing the course final project report. They write a paper analyzing the strengths of the teaching they observed, make suggestions where there is room for improvement, establish connections to theory on best teaching practices, and draw implications for practice. This class activity allows everybody to learn from each other, teachers, learners and

Table 8.1 Elements to consider in an ESL classroom observation

Required for the university classroom	Suggested by the literature
(1) Instructors' content knowledge, organization and evidence of preparedness to teach the lesson	(1) Knowledge of adult learning and second language acquisition
(2) Rapport between instructor and students, and relationships among students	(2) Awareness of learners' styles, disabilities and learning needs
(3) Teaching method, approach, style and philosophy	(3) Authentic assessment of learning needs
(4) Presentation of concepts	(4) Drawing on learners' prior experiences
(5) Time management	(5) Relevant content, immediately usable to the learner
(6) Sensitivity to students' cultural differences, and assistance provided to students to complete tasks	(6) Involvement of learners in planning instruction
(7) Personal and professional self-confidence	(7) Schedule and intensity of the course to fit learners' needs (Orem, 2005: 64–65)
(8) Physical aspect of the classroom	

teacher-learners (Elwell & Bean, 2001; Stanton *et al.*, 1999). To honor the principles of engaged scholarship and critical reflection, the teacher-learners share their learning with the instructors they observe by having an informal dialogue with them and reporting what they see as strengths and possibilities for improvement. In addition, during class time at the university, there is discussion on the notes made from the observations and the teacher-learners' reflective journal entries. For example, Marissa, born in the United States, shared the following from her journal:

> Watching two different classes in the same ESL program made me think about my own teaching style. Both instructors held solid connections with their students. Their classroom environments felt open and safe, which is exactly how I want my own classroom to feel. The first class I observed was an ESL writing class, which was considered a beginner class, but is actually multilevel. The students have a wide range of English background, which was evident in their reading and writing ability. I was surprised as to how little writing was actually being practiced in the classroom. It didn't seem like they were asked to write paragraphs as much as just sentences. Many of the more advanced students were waiting around for others to finish, so, maybe in that case, I would have had them extend their writing to a paragraph, just for more practice. Also surprising was how quickly the class covered 'the writing process', which was about the last ten minutes of class! The discussion of prewriting, the options of how to write an essay, practice writing, thesis statements, these are all part of the process and I would think need a good day for discussion. I definitely would have liked to see more of the writing aspect for the writing class. Overall, the class was full of learning opportunities, which the instructor made sure to explain, but I believe that time management could have been the culprit in not getting enough writing in for the students. Planning is essential!
>
> On the other hand, the reading class I observed was planned very efficiently. Even when the conversations seemed to get a little off topic the

instructor would still swing the conversation back to the subject matter. Every project in the class, from reviewing the homework to the quiz, had a reading component. The students felt comfortable discussing situations from their home countries that related to the readings in class. It was refreshing to see the students engaged and discussing freely their thoughts, concerns and 'putting their two-cents in'. The class was a controlled, open forum for discussion. Again, this goes back to the safe environment the students felt that they were in, so this feeling of acceptance and safety seems to be very important in an ESL classroom.

As illustrated by Marissa's journal entry, the objective of the assignment was accomplished. Similarly, Udall *et al.* (2015) suggests, 'real value is placed on the importance of practical experience, and of developing (both in terms of mind and action) through the understanding of those practical experiences' (2015: 168). Marissa was able to see actual TESOL instructors in action and was able to reflect on how she wants her classroom to be. She gives emphasis to the importance of having a lesson plan to follow and the relevance of good time management skills while delivering a lesson. Using a constructive criticism approach, Marissa can put herself in the shoes of the two instructors she observed. Ideally, the teacher-learner would observe the same TESOL instructor to be able to compare what happened on different days. Owing to time constraints and other real-life factors, they may end up observing two different instructors. However, they still have to meet with the instructor and discuss the observation to complete the exercise.

Pat, also from the United States, noted in her journal that:

> Quality ESL lesson planning is the key to trigger learners' success. If students are engaged and they understand what is happening in the lesson, they are able and willing to participate. The implementation of the lesson plan is the core of ESL teaching. The teacher can have a good lesson plan but can fail to execute it. This requires practice. I want to be one of those teachers who are able to make realistic lesson plans. I want to keep in mind the students' learning needs and the program teaching needs. In addition, teachers should restate the goals for the next class. This will help build continuity. The students will have present in their minds what comes next and be mentally prepared for the next lesson. These are the areas where I see the instructor I observed needs to make improvements.

In this journal entry, Pat addresses the reality of designing lesson plans; the instructor may have a good lesson plan but fail in the delivery of the lesson. Going from paper to reality requires experience. As Freire (2001) explained: 'To teach is not to *transfer knowledge* but to create the possibilities for the production or construction of knowledge' (2001: 30).

Knowing the theory or having a well-designed lesson plan is not enough. Many factors influence the lesson (e.g. audience, flexibility of the lesson plan, relevance of the topic, learner engagement, appropriate learning objectives, time management, visual aids, plenty of student practice, learning extension, and assessment). On a related topic, Aleena, from the Middle East, added that:

> The ESL teacher I observed showed great sensitivity to his students. He tried to make them feel comfortable and create a nice learning environment; however, I noticed something that I am not sure he realized. He paired up a Muslim male student with a female Mexican student for a role play exercise. Due to religious and cultural considerations, it is possible that this might have been an uncomfortable situation for the Muslim student. It is very important for language teachers to be more knowledgeable of their students' cultures to avoid conflict and show respect to the students' cultural traditions. Another issue was that the teacher seemed too worried to create a positive learning environment at the cost of providing effective feedback on student performance. I would advise her to provide more feedback for students to be able to reflect and correct their language production mistakes. The students need to be able to learn from their mistakes.

In her journal entry, Aleena points out the importance of knowing the basics about the cultural traditions and rules of the students' cultures. This may help to avoid conflict and show sensitivity to these situations. She was able to detect this incident because she understands the culture; however, the course instructor may not be aware. Orem (2005: 79) adds that teachers of adult English learners need to have a positive attitude toward the learners and the learner's home language and culture. This positive attitude needs to be supported by actual knowledge of the cultures represented in the classroom. Asking the learners directly about what makes them feel uncomfortable in relation to cultural norms is an efficient way to approach this learning of other cultures.

Tutoring adult English learners

Flyers were sent to ESL programs in the area serving adult learners asking for motivated students who would like to do extra practice. This activity is implemented during class time so that the teacher-learners have a chance to experience teaching English one-on-one to a variety of adult learners (see Figure 8.1). It is common not to know who is going to show up to the tutoring sessions and that adds another level of challenge to the activity. This is necessary practice for the teacher-learners to develop the ability to quickly build rapport and be prepared to teach whoever shows up for class. During the five weeks that this project lasts,

Figure 8.1 Learner in a tutoring session

the teacher-learners are required to keep a journal to reflect about what works and what needs improvement during their tutoring sessions. Haashim, a Muslim graduate student, noted the following in his journal:

> My first tutoring experience was with Robin, a Chinese student. His major goals included practicing speaking and expressing himself in a variety of real-life circumstances. He spoke about his life in China, in particular Chinese holidays and celebrations comparing them to the American ones.
>
> During the second session, two female students from Saudi Arabia, Chin and Alaa, were assigned to me, and Robin didn't come. He came back for the next three sessions. Chin and Alaa both had desire for improving their abilities in expressing opinions and develop speaking skills. This session involved a variety of topics and games. Using games was a very good idea to encourage them to speak. We did a dice game to express personal feelings about some topics. I felt more prepared this time to do the tutoring session, and I was not as nervous as the first time.
>
> Some challenges during the tutoring sessions included the individual differences in backgrounds, the learners' native languages, and cultures. However, planning for meaningful interaction and the development of vocabulary helped. The learners came back, and that was a success for me. As the instructor, I have to show confidence to instill it in the learners, too.

Haashim makes several good points in his reflection. Being prepared and showing confidence are two important traits in a TESOL instructor. Freire (2001: 85) highlights that 'the self-confident authority with which the teacher is imbued implies another type of self-confidence that's grounded in professional competence'. If they are prepared, they will be organized, have good time management and be able to show self-confidence. Haashim was also from the Middle East, so interacting with Chin and Alaa was relatively easy for him; however, Robin was from China. This helped Haashim reflect on the role of cultural differences in the classroom dynamics.

In relation to his experience tutoring adult English learners, another teacher-learner spoke about the need to be prepared, have a variety of activities planned, and build rapport with the learners. Julio, a Mexican-American graduate student, wrote in his journal:

> Exactly one thing that I learned is that I have to prepare ahead of time. I needed to have different types of activities to adjust to the students' needs. In establishing a good rapport with the students, I was able to informally communicate with them. The students came in ready and willing to learn more English, and they saw me as a resource. The tutoring sessions were important because they prepared me for my internship in the next semester.

For some master's students this was their first time teaching a real-life adult English learner. This project gave them a chance to test their teaching skills and plan for improvement for the near future. Similarly, Jenny, from the United States stated that:

> Examining what was meaningful to my own learning made me think of the possibilities I can create while teaching ESL to adults. I would like to find out more about my students' learning stories from day one. This tutoring experience has made me aware of the various backgrounds adult learners may come from and with this knowledge, I need to plan to be more culturally sensitive when planning the lessons.

All of the teacher-learners spoke about the need to get to know their students' learning needs and cultural backgrounds to make good lesson planning decisions. The learners that the teacher-learners worked with inspired them to continue learning about the profession.

Serving as conversation partners

For this project, adult English learners from two local TESOL programs who wanted to have a conversation partner for 10 weeks were the target audience. The focus of the project was helping adult learners develop oral language fluency and practice conversation. The teacher-learners had a chance to plan lessons for teaching conversation and reflect on how well they implemented these lessons. Most of the teacher-learners commented on overcoming their fear of not being able to do a good job as conversation partners/instructors and the strong bonds they built with the ESL learners. Here is what Bob, Nancy and Albert shared in their reflection journal entries:

Bob: I over prepared with activities at first. But then, I mapped out a plan and was more aware of the allotted time and the learners' needs. Overall, this was a very positive experience and I plan on keeping in touch with my student to continue helping her with her English development. I will continue to volunteer.

Nancy: At first, I was apprehensive as to whether or not I would be able to do a good job teaching ESL conversation. Additionally, I was quite concerned about not having a well-established lesson plan to follow, but quickly discovered, I needed to determine what works best for my student first. Looking back, the experience was quite rewarding and reminded me once more why I am into teaching ... seeing the excitement in students when they learn something that is important and meaningful to their lives. This experience really highlighted for me what it means to allow the student to 'inform what is to be learned'. Allowing the student to 'shape' the learning process really allowed her to feel engaged and empowered.

Albert: I was able to develop a strong relationship with the learner I was working with. She did not miss a class although she was late once or twice. She followed through on her commitments and the trust within the relationship also started to grow with each passing session. The learner became more open about her life, life complications, work and dreams. I was also able to help her with specific language skills.

The teacher-learners spoke about the importance of being good listeners to become good conversation partners and instructors. The learners they were serving taught lessons to the teacher-learners that they could simply not have been able to learn sitting in the graduate classrooms discussing theory (Elwell & Bean, 2001). The teacher-learners also mentioned important tips they discovered about how to improve their own practice. They all expressed how much they enjoyed the experience of meeting new people to have a conversation with. Here is what Cecilia, Ellen and George had to say:

Cecilia: The partnership I built with my participant allowed us to engage in great conversation. I am happy that I was able to receive a student with whom I was able to connect and enjoy great conversation. My interaction with the learner was more of a collaborative partnership rather than a traditional student–teacher relationship. I learned that I have strong influence over conversation, setting, and interaction with the learner. Therefore, at times, my personality allowed me to continue a conversation, but other times my desire to comment and speak caused interference with the learner's space and time to tell their story. I continue telling myself that I should be an active listener, not over-correct the learner, be engaging and have fun.

Ellen: It was a fun experience. I didn't know what to expect as I have never worked with an adult English learner. So, I went in with an open mind and was surprised how fun the project was and how I was able to have some rather interesting conversations with my student. I talk a lot. I need to learn to be more of a listener and stop inserting myself into the conversation.

George: I had a great time getting to know my participant. We both shared quite a bit about our families and the things that we love. Confidence is a key factor in engaging in conversational English, on both ends. Listening is very important too, especially to provide space for practice for the learner.

Congruent with Udall *et al.*'s (2015) findings, 'throwing university students into unfamiliar territory where they are forced to draw on their resources far beyond anything written into a curriculum benefits them; a huge amount of intense "experience" is gained in a very short space of time' (2015: 168). In this case, participating in learning events such as classroom observations, tutoring adult English learners and serving as conversation partners for adult English learners were learning opportunities that made the student-teachers grow in confidence and professional competence, and allowed them to reflect on what good teaching should look like.

Learning from internship practices

In an internship, the teacher-learners are placed as trainees at different adult education organizations to gain experience, network with future colleagues and continue learning in the real world. This section provides narratives of their experiences while participating in a semester-long internship. The interns keep a journal and write observations and reflections about their experiences at the internship sites. The journal also serves as a space for the teacher-learners to examine their emotions and preconceived notions about the realities of teaching ESOL learners. The following narrative provides a concise summary of the first four days of the internship experience of Amari.

The first day of the internship was extremely overwhelming. It was my first time to be in an adult class with students who are almost twice my age. Even the location of the center, in the east side of the city, did not give me the best impression. It was in a neighborhood that doesn't seem to be safe. To be honest, I was a little uncomfortable, maybe even scared to be in such place. I know I picked the organization, but I didn't know they were going to send me here to the poor side of the city.

The learners were from diverse ethnic backgrounds ... races and backgrounds that I am not very familiar with and have never had any related experiences in the past. The entire environment was not very appealing, and I thought of finding another place to do internship. But I decided to stay and gain experience.

I felt a little better the second day of class. I got used to the learners who were very nice and kind. They appreciated any help offered to them. Then, my onsite mentor's teaching style proved challenging as well. Ms. Kerry just gave each student a packet suitable to their level. There was not actual instruction or even directions. These were workbooks with exercises to prepare for the GED test. It seemed like everybody knew what was going on but me! So, I observed and asked her what was expected of me. Teacher Kerry explained that I needed to wait for students to ask for help. At the beginning, they were a little shy to call for me since I was new to them. Therefore, I tried to remove this barrier and approached them whenever possible. During the third class, they were very comfortable asking for my help.

By the fourth class, I was almost helping all students. I started to feel more and more comfortable around the learners and at the center. I was assigned to help one of the students who is an ESL learner. She is an immigrant who came from Iraq and was trying to get her GED diploma to go to the community college. She was practicing advanced reading skills from the book *Top 50 Reading Skills for GED Success*. It was not an easy book for me to help her without having prior knowledge. Ms. Kerry hadn't informed me about this book, plus that every student is working on something different. I did my best to help the learner, but sometimes my choices for inference and drawing conclusion were not right because I had to read the entire passage in a few seconds and know the answer. It was even hard for Ms. Kerry to help, she would sit and read the entire passage first. I took the book home, read it, and was prepared to help. I wasn't sure about the exact page number where the learner was because every day she does whatever she can. Ms. Kerry couldn't anticipate what section she will be doing the next class. Therefore, I took the challenge and read the whole book at home to be ready to help that advanced learner.

On the fifth week, the students were very comfortable asking for my help. Then, the students who were doing math thought I could help them and started asking for help. Even though it was beginner math, it was hard to explain it to them in an easy way. I spent about two weeks until I was able to master all the math problems the learners were doing.

When I thought everything was under control, one day I went to class as usual, but Ms. Kerry was not there. I started helping the students as usual. After almost an hour, one of the administrators from the center came with some envelopes and said to the learners 'I have some news for you, teacher Kerry left'. Then, the administrator handed each one a letter that she wrote to them. Each student opened their envelope and read the letter. I saw a smile on the face of all of them. According to them the letter was to encourage them to continue to work hard. She really cared for them!

The following week, there was a new teacher. We were all a little uncomfortable. The students missed Ms. Kerry; I've worked with her for two months, so I missed her too. But, gradually, we all got used to the new teacher and her teaching style.

This narrative shared by Amari allows the readers to consider the teacher-learner's point of view and the process of settling into the internship site. This intern in particular was not familiar with how adult education classes worked at the organization where he was doing his internship practice. Thus, on the first day at the learning center where Amari was assigned, everything seemed strange and overwhelming.

Leaving the comfort of the university classroom to face real-life conditions under which learners in the community attend adult education programs may be a shocking experience at first. As Udall *et al.* (2015) suggested, 'the process of getting to know one another provided an important part of the learning' (2015: 162). Teacher-learners need to realize that the adult education classroom is made up of diverse ethnicities, cultures, and languages. These are not heterogeneous groups, and they must learn both how to interact with everybody in the classroom and how to help these adults achieve their learning goals.

Another important fact from this narrative is that all teachers, novice and expert, need to continue to study and prepare for providing high-quality education and mastering content knowledge. As Freire (2001) explained, 'Teachers who do not take their own education seriously, who do not study, who make little effort to keep abreast of events have no moral authority to coordinate the activities of the classroom' (2001: 85). In the case of Amari, it was important to understand how to teach reading comprehension, learn the teaching material and be prepared to be able to assist the learners with their questions. Studying beyond his university course and preparing for real-life teaching helped him feel confident and competent. In the end, it was a good experience for all; Amari, the ESL and GED learners, and their teachers were able to work together and learn from each other.

Conclusion

The stories provided by the teacher-learners can inspire other teachers and volunteer instructors who are seeking professional development to improve their TESOL practices. These narratives illustrated that engaged scholarship could be a door to collaboration, professional growth and reciprocal learning. Through volunteering to be tutors, serving as conversation partners or participating in internships, novice teachers could learn about the challenges that ESL learners experience trying to attend instruction and succeed at learning English. The theory provided in the university classroom is important; however, this theory must come to life through practice. As Udall *et al.* (2015) state, 'the "real-life" experiences outlined by these projects could simply never be re-created in a classroom environment' (2015: 169). Therefore, when training teacher-learners, it is very important to provide opportunities for them to participate in actual teaching. Participating in real-life teaching situations such as the ones described in this chapter is an important learning experience to build confidence in becoming effective TESOL instructors. Another significant issue is to require teacher-learners to constantly reflect on their teaching practices. Keeping a reflection journal is an essential practice that they could continue to use throughout their careers.

Recommendations for Practice

(1) Imagine alternative options to teacher development (e.g. create opportunities for observing other colleagues' teaching, discuss your observations and learn from other instructors).
(2) Engage as a teacher-learner in a context other than the university classroom (e.g. participate in a book club for ESL learner, join a conversation club to teach speaking, etc.).
(3) Start a reflection journal to examine what works and what does not work when teaching adult English learners. Review the journal periodically and outline a plan of action for improving your teaching.
(4) Share your knowledge with colleagues and have conversations with them about best teaching practices.
(5) Subscribe and participate in professional organizations and list-serves (e.g. TESOL International, COABE, LRA and NCTE) to keep current on the news and trends related to teaching ESOL learners.

Discussion Questions (Group Activity)

(1) What are the benefits of keeping a reflective journal analyzing your teaching practices?
(2) What advice would you give to a novice TESOL instructor to succeed in the profession?
(3) What can a novice ESL teacher learn from participating in class observations?
(4) What are other ideas you can think of to help novice teachers understand the realities of adult ESL programs (e.g. funding issues, curriculum, policies and job remuneration)?

9 Negotiating Adult ESL Curriculum

Negotiating the Curriculum

A negotiation approach to teaching and learning requires the teacher to include the students in the process of designing and implementing the curriculum (Ahlstrom, 2003; Boomer et al., 1992; Cook, 1992; Harris, 2010). This process involves 'deliberately planning to invite students to contribute to, and to modify, the educational program, so that they will have real investment both in the learning journey and in the outcomes' (Boomer et al., 1992: 14). Overall, curriculum negotiation refers to providing the learners with the possibility of making decisions and changes to the lesson plan. In such a learner-centered classroom, 'learners are active participants in their own learning, rather than passive objects to be manipulated' (Nunan, 2015: 19). Often, the students know why they need to learn L2 and have clear personal motivations, but they do not know how to accomplish these goals besides enrolling in language classes. Similarly, Nunan (2015) states that 'some learners have clear ideas about what they want to learn and how they want to learn; however, many do not. It's for this reason we need to begin helping them to take control of their own learning' (2015: 24). Through curriculum negotiation, they can assume responsibility of their own learning and still have guidance from their teachers.

The learners must be aware of the requirements of the program where they are enrolled because 'negotiation also means making explicit, and then confronting, the constraints of the learning context and the non-negotiable requirements that apply' (Boomer et al., 1992: 14). In other words, in curriculum negotiation, both parties need to be aware of the context and the program requirements, the teacher's needs and the learners' needs. Whitmore and Crowell (1994) agree and recommend that the teacher draw boundaries for negotiation based on their professional experiences. Even though communication is the primary focus in any adult ESL program, grammar teaching also plays an important role. Thus, the teacher can work on grammar 'within the context of the themes brought out by the students … addressing grammar in its role as an aid to effective communication' (Ahlstrom, 2003: 3). Grammar is an essential component of L2 and a non-negotiable component of the curriculum. Likewise, establishing negotiation boundaries in adult education translates to observing federal government policies and fulfilling requirements imposed by funders. For example, being able to show data supporting student progress and program success (e.g. enrollment data, test scores, adults becoming economically self-sufficient) is a requirement for these programs.

In adult ESL teaching, curriculum negotiation is a democratic activity since it presents students with an opportunity to voice their concerns and make choices about what and how to learn (Breen & Littlejohn, 2000; Harris, 2010; Nguyen, 2011; Nunan, 2015). Teaching and learning in dialogue make the adult classroom a social setting where participants are jointly responsible for the learning that takes place (Freire, 1970). The goal of curriculum negotiation is to make teaching more responsive to learners' needs, increase their involvement in learning, enhance their confidence, develop autonomy and learning responsibility, and build a mutual understanding between teacher and learners (Breen & Littlejohn, 2000; Harris, 2010; Nguyen, 2011). Ahlstrom (2003) argues that teachers should not get carried away creating curriculum thinking that as teachers they know best; the right approach would be 'to pose the question to the students and brainstorm ideas so they could collaboratively reach solutions' (2003: 3). The students can surprise the teacher with their creativity and preferences as to how to approach a situation using their unique position as immigrants and adult learners (Freire, 1970). From this point of view, curriculum negotiation refers to providing the learners with the possibility of making decisions and changes to the lesson plan and program while also taking responsibility for their own learning.

Becoming an Adult ESL Teacher

After graduation, a large adult education organization was hiring instructors; I was hired as an English teacher, an ESL teacher. I started teaching two nights a week at the public library and as an adjunct at two local universities. I ended up getting hooked up with the intensive English program and taught English there. I was also an ESL tutor tutoring for Japanese students who wanted admission to the local university. It wasn't until my 8th year working as a part-timer with the adult education organization that I finally went full-time. Somebody retired at AELC [Adult Education Learning Center], and I was able to get a full-time job.

I have been working for the AELC for five years now. I was finally able to quit my many jobs! Working as an adjunct instructor doesn't pay much. Still today, the way to survive and pay the bills is by teaching a couple of hours here, a couple of hours there. And that's the situation of most of our teachers at AELC as well. A lot of them are retired teachers who just teach a few hours. Others are young folks without families and come from different careers. Others are teachers in the school district who are single; they work for us in the evening and the school district during the day.

Abby describes the precarious work conditions for educators who work at publicly funded adult education organizations (see Figure 9.1). Teachers often need to hold multiple jobs and 'many teachers are part-time employees often without the security of tenure' (Brown & Bywater, 2009/2010: 203). Unfortunately, this is the reality of adult ESL teaching across the nation (Center for Applied Linguistics, 2010).

Often, ESL instructors' preparation and credentials vary, from having TESOL training or a degree in Adult Education to holding degrees from other disciplines (e.g. Curriculum and Instruction, Communication Studies, Psychology, Counseling and Business) or a TESOL certificate (Brown & Bywater, 2009/2010; Larrotta *et al.*, 2016). Most of the time, ESL instructors have learned the profession while on the job and through professional development or by following advice from experienced colleagues. These work conditions create a disadvantage and generate barriers for curriculum negotiation. When working so many jobs, it is difficult to know the concerns of the learners, and teachers barely get to know their students personally or the workings of their programs since they are busy running back and forth to different campuses (Brown & Bywater, 2009/2010). Curriculum negotiation is student centered and reading the classroom dynamics, as suggested by Ahlstrom

Figure 9.1 Abby teaching a class

(2003), may not be as easy as it sounds. Next, Abby describes her professional background:

> My degree was in communication studies with an emphasis on interpersonal communication. It was a business communication degree. That's where the money is; the graduates go into consulting, training, and organizations. But, obviously, that was not my path. Teaching adults is a great job really. To me, it's a great job! Cuz a lot of what we do is counseling. I took some graduate classes on communication in the classroom and communication in small groups. Most divorces and conflict are due to not knowing how to communicate. We don't know how to listen, how to be sensitive, or take responsibility for our words. This is what I do most of the time, not just teach English. It's teaching people to communicate, and it's also teaching people to reflect on their lives. When you deal with people in poverty, they lack a lot of life skills. They need guidance on how to become aware of what they can do interpersonally so they can better their situation. No longer blame their partners or the external factors ... So, I know how to communicate, and I care about my students on an individual level. I'm genuinely interested in their lives and in their successes and in their personal growth. I'm positive and encouraging; I help them feel safe and they enjoy coming. It's not a burden.

Abby relies on her university training in communication studies to conduct her classes when working with adults and immigrants. She practices what Ahlstrom (2003) calls 'emergent theme-based curriculum' since Abby listens to the learners in her class and provides the space for them to have conversations about topics such as divorce, women's independence, losing a parent, leaving the homeland, educating children, violence and trauma that the learners experience as immigrants and women. Abby uses her professional knowledge in communication studies and ESL teaching to shape the way she runs the curriculum. Her students are not aware that they are negotiating the curriculum, and Abby's practice seems to follow a tacit negotiation of the ESL curriculum by listening to their stories to then select topics for class discussion and dialogue.

Services Offered to Adult Learners

Adult education programs seldom provide only language and literacy instruction. Rather, the end goal is to prepare adults to live as self-reliant individuals and provide access to information that they need for success in their roles as parents, employees, consumers and lifelong learners (Brown & Bywater, 2009/2010; Center for Applied Linguistics, 2010; Milana & McBain, 2014). In this case, AELC operates from a one-story building with three large rooms for classes. The first classroom doubles up as the computer room. The second classroom also functions as an office or reception. The last classroom is the smallest. In addition, there is not an actual library; instead, they have several bookshelves with dictionaries, textbooks and reading materials around the walls of the largest classroom. Parking spaces are scarce as well. They have six instructors teaching onsite and a few others working part-time teaching at the public library and the local high school. Regardless of the lack of space and resources, AELC offers many programs and serves a large number of adult learners. Abby shared the following during the interview:

> At AELC, we're currently offering Spanish GED, regular GED, ESL classes, and computer classes. Due to space limitations, we offered several ESL courses at the high school next door, and we have an advanced ESL class being offered at the public library in a neighboring city. Here at our location, we are offering an entrepreneurial class; we're teaching adults in the community about opening their own businesses. We offer citizenship preparation as well. We're not really calling that one a class; we have someone there to help the students with their applications and practice the interview questions, but there's not going to be a lesson taught. It's a service we're going to have this year. People are asking for that class, but realistically, there's no funding. We're providing this service because we believe it does help them. Last year, we offered a structured class for one hour a week, and people in the community wanted us to offer it again this year. A lot of people call about it, but this is all we can do. We don't have a test or materials to really have an actual class on the citizenship test. I think TWC, the Texas Workforce Commission, is moving forward with that, if it helps them more, but at this point, it's not funded. So we're offering it as an extra bonus. We're somewhat in transition because of TWC. They want us to provide certifications to help the students get a job. It's all about moving them into employment, such as electrician, welding, whatever the high demand occupations are for this area. They're willing to help pay for high demand occupation certifications.

As Abby explained, TWC prioritizes transitioning adult learners to the workplace as quickly as possible. According to their website (http://www.twc.state.tx.us/students), adult education and literacy programs should help students acquire the skills needed to succeed in the workforce, earn a high school equivalency, or enter college or career training. Thus, as the funder, TWC is establishing the boundaries for curriculum negotiation. In other words, based on these demands, Abby's program will identify the skills that the learners need to acquire, and the teachers could ask for student input so that 'specific skills and competencies are taught using student-generated topics of interest' (Carver, 2003: 36). This seems to be the reality of adult education programs when instruction is offered for free and is government funded.

Enrollment and Completion Issues

It is difficult to identify one single factor or barrier to participation in adult education. A report by the Center for Applied Linguistics (2010) identified several factors impacting learner participation in adult education programs:

> Learner factors include work schedules, family responsibilities, opportunities to learn and use English outside of an instructional setting, marital and family status, and personal motivation. Program factors include availability of classes, class schedules and locations, instructional setting, type of entry into the program (open or managed enrollment), length of courses and frequency of classes, and training and expertise of the teacher. (2010: viii)

Likewise, the section below describes the enrollment and attrition issues that Abby's program faces every year. She explains why they offer so many services and reports on the large demand for adult education services.

> During the year, we offer three orientation meetings to inform people about the program. If our classes start dropping off, we'll do an extra one in October and another in January. We could have 50 people attending one night and another 25 attending the following night just for the orientation. We have a big demand and large classes, but still need more students to comply with the funder requirements. Each semester, in the ESL program, we serve 60 students who complete the courses. At the orientation, we have around 150 people wanting ESL classes, but half of them show up and finish in the ESL program annually. For example, last year in my morning class, I was teaching ESL 2, I had 25 students, and 20 of those finished the course. For GED, 100 people showed up for the orientation and only 50 came in for the GED classes. Of those, I would say 20 in GED completed more than 12 hours. That's how we in our program do the count. They're counted as a student once they have completed more than 12 hours, but we count progress at 40 hours for GED and 60 for ESL. So to show gain and receive funding, we need for students to complete 40 hours for GED, and 60 for ESL. They need to make it to the end of the year. It's a problem. Some years are good, and some years are bad. Typically, when the economy is doing well, the students don't stay as much because they get jobs. When the economy is bad, our enrollment numbers are up because they have time; they can't find a job.

Abby explains that student participation in the ESL program relates to the course level. Thus, in ESL level 1, more students drop out every year. Her rationale about why the students in level 1 drop out of the program more often illustrates her awareness of the need to build community in the ESL classroom.

> ESL level 1 is more difficult for them! Maybe because there's so much that they have to learn. They get overwhelmed, and it's harder for them to commit because they don't see their progress as fast as they would like it to happen. I guess that's another factor to think about. Depending on the level, the students persist or finish their course in larger numbers. Also, it depends on their English skills; if their language level is really low or really high, it does make a difference in participation. If they have a high

level, they can survive. So studying English is not as much of a necessity for them anymore. They can go to the bank; they can go to the supermarket. So they don't commit as much. It's that middle group who want to commit to attend the classes, the ones who speak a little bit, so they really see themselves progressing ... Last year, I had a very special group of women. They were very close-knit. Already 12 of them have registered for level 3 this year. Ten have registered for level 3 and two have registered to return to my level, level 2. I'm not sure if it has to do with using WhatsApp? This is the first year we have used that as a group to do texting outside of class, and so that built some connection.

Abby keeps in touch with her students after work hours through texting and voicemail. Using WhatsApp, a voicemail and text application, allows the students to communicate with her and their classmates outside of class. Using WhatsApp means having extra practice in dialogue with each other and practicing L2 while building community outside of class. Abby continues to elaborate on this issue:

The adults attending classes at the learning center have similar life experiences and struggles. Once they get to know each other and the staff working at the center, they feel supported and safe. Most don't know anyone else but family. They have no friends. It's a community center, but also, I believe they really feel like they're learning English in a safe place where they are valued as people. They see themselves improve, and there's a lot of encouragement.

Likewise, a study by Buttaro and King (2001) found that program involvement, especially teacher involvement, positively influences learners' English performance. When adult learners feel that they belong to a place (e.g. the ESL classroom and the literacy program they are attending), they invest in their learning, stay enrolled in class and feel committed to help each other learn. Nunan (2015) also reminds us that 'in a learner-centered classroom, learning experiences are related to learners' own out-of-class experiences' (2015: 19).

When All in Class are Female

Below, Abby describes the student body in her classroom. She also identifies the commonalities that she enjoys and shares with her students when all those in the class are female.

I teach ESL level 2 or intermediate ESL in the morning, from 9:00 am to 12 noon. Most of my students are from Central America, and some are from South America. Almost all are low-income, and I'd say 50% are undocumented. In the morning program, most of the students are women ages 28 to 45. The population is different in the morning than the evening. The evening is mainly people who have jobs, and 70% of them are men. For the morning classes, the women are typically parents, so their kids are at school; they are stay at home moms. Some are grandparents;

the oldest student I have is 78. Most of my students have only been educated to the sixth-grade math level. Occasionally to the ninth grade, some only until the third grade. This year my class was made up of 24 female students and 1 male student who came sporadically. Family is very important to them, and to me; I really value that part of the Latin culture, and so I learn a lot from them, like cooking, and sewing, which are not my strengths! When all of us in class are women, I feel like they're able to open-up more. As women, mothers, immigrants, and some undocumented, they have hard lives but it's all very interesting!

As Isserlis (2000) states, 'Immigrant women suffer a triple burden of discrimination based on their sex, race, and immigration status' (2000: 2). Once they start learning about the new culture, it is inevitable for students to compare it with their own. This can create what scholars call a disorienting dilemma (Mezirow & Associates, 1990), which is an internal or external personal crisis and Abby speaks about this phenomenon:

> Over the years, I've seen that when married couples move here, and typically they're from Hispanic cultures, it's very hard for the marriage. The husbands are used to having a lot of control and dominance over their wives. However, here the women do not stay home; they come to the learning center to study. There are all these opportunities for women. We encouraged them to be independent and strong and most of these women start having an identity crisis. They don't know where they fit anymore. Their husbands are working 12 or 13 hours out in construction. So, I think that is how women end up coming to class. But then, the husbands see their wives' progress and becoming more assimilated to the culture, and it becomes a source of conflict. There is a lot of divorce and a lot of conflict once they come to the U.S. These are people who have been married for 20, 30 years. So, in class, these women find the space to open-up about that kind of stuff because it's all women attending class. The class becomes an outlet for therapy. They want to talk about their issues. They want to listen to other opinions. They want to tell their stories. Even if the problem won't be solved, they want to feel encouraged, and they want to hear that they are going to survive these crises.

As is the case in Abby's class, sociopolitical and cultural adjustment issues find their way into adult ESL classes as the learners work to make sense of the new language and culture (Buttaro & King, 2001). Most adult immigrants experience trauma, psychological acculturation and specific transition stages while adapting to their new communities and integrating into the workforce in a new country (Akhtar, 2011; American Psychological Association, Presidential Task Force on Immigration, 2012; Tummala-Narra, 2014). Thus, the ESL class becomes an outlet for them to vent and reflect on their life experiences. In this case, Abby's students learn about the different roles and possibilities that women have in US culture and realize this is something they would like for themselves. However, their families and/or cultural traditions may conflict with this new viewpoint.

Abby continues to discuss how their status as immigrant women affects the students' learning:

> To me, learning can't go on, real learning and change can't go on if they're not at peace. The brain can't really change and receive new knowledge until they're relaxed. So, it's a big deal for me. I spend weeks and months building relationships. I want the students to care about each other. I care about them. I would say that 60% of the teaching has to do with creating community ... The content is maybe the other 40%, but I could be teaching the best stuff, and if that's not going on, they're not going to come back. They're not really going to be listening and learning. They are not going to go tell their friends about my class, about the center. Why would they go tell someone if they don't enjoy coming, and why would they spend three hours a day, four days a week, twelve hours a week with me in class? I can't even commit to one hour of exercise a week. Here are people committing 3 hours a day ... it's gotta be something that's more than just learning language.

Existing research supports Abby's assertions 'since language learning demands control, connection, and meaning, adults experiencing effects of past or current trauma are particularly challenged in learning a new language' (Isserlis, 2000: 3). In promoting community building, Abby creates the space for the learners to open up and share their preoccupations and questions. After all, in curriculum negotiation, the main goal is to teach relevant topics that reflect the life experiences and learning needs of adult English learners. Thus, Abby's narrative aligns with curriculum negotiation as she envisions the learners as partners in their own educational journey (Ahlstrom, 2003; Carver, 2003; Harris, 2010; Nguyen, 2011). For example, she emphasizes that relationship building is important to keep students coming back to class. If students feel connected to their classmates and teacher and if they feel they are viewed as people, not just a number or a score to get funding, they will be able to relate to one another, feel safe and be open to new learning.

So far, Abby's negotiation of the ESL curriculum has emerged according to her 'reading of the class dynamics' and dialogue practices. To this effect, Ahlstrom (2003) suggests discovering themes that are interesting or important to 'gain ideas informally, noticing which topics engage students emotionally' (2003: 4). Curriculum negotiation with adult ESL learners then takes shape through student-generated topics which spark discussion and encourage them to share other related experiences, give advice and suggestions to each other, and keep dialogue alive in the classroom. In turn, in the spirit of dialogue, Freire has labeled these as 'generative themes'. Generative themes 'contain the possibility of unfolding into ... as many themes, which in turn would call for new tasks to be fulfilled' (Freire, 1970: 102). Generative themes are complex topics, central to adults' lives, and serve to express their viewpoints about the world as immigrants and learners. Using these themes, the participants engage in authentic dialogue to learn about each other's reality and construct a more comprehensive view of a topic, the host community and the world. Next, Abby continues to report on other aspects that make her students' lives more complex:

> Some of these women have lost a relative, or their parents back in their countries of origin, and they want to hear from other people that have lost their parents. They are in that stage where their parents are getting sick and dying. I mean, most our students are in an age that their own parents are older, and they are back home. Some of them, undocumented, haven't seen their parents in 15 years and can't go back. So, they're heartbroken. They moved here to give their kids an opportunity, and they're losing a very big part of themselves. So, they get support even if we are not able to solve a lot of the issues. However, there is support for them in our program. Then, the class content and discussion topics change because of what they're interested in and what they need.
>
> A lot of them have been in the U.S. for 20 years and have not learned English. Their kids are now grown, and they have a chance to go back and try to study the language. So, part of it is with speaking the language, and the other part is typically about poverty. If you go drive over on the East side, many of the places where they live don't have sewage, for example. People are dumping black water on the street. There are 10–15 people living in a two-bedroom mobile home. They have people being shot next door or fighting, domestic violence going on, or their own kids are into drugs and gangs, and they don't know how to help them, so there's also the safety that they can come and learn and not be worried about being deported. They can experience and learn about multiple levels of safety here at the learning center.

Often, participation in ESL classes positively affects female adult learners' linguistic, cultural and educational adjustment. Accordingly, in agreement with curriculum negotiation principles, the teacher should create an environment that fosters self-esteem, a sense of safety and an interest in learning (Breen & Littlejohn, 2000; Harris, 2010; Nguyen, 2011). As Abby explained, the ESL class will not offer the solutions to all their problems, but the learners should be able to acquire important tools such as communication strategies to share feelings, ideas and doubts with other people. Above all, they should feel safe and engaged in learning (Buttaro & King, 2001).

As Abby mentioned during the interview, in the ESL classroom the students can learn about multiple levels of safety. However, they bring up many different issues to address in a short period of time. Even though they are all immigrants and female, it does not necessarily mean that they all share the same experience or have the same level of interest about these various topics. Ahlstrom (2003) offers an appropriate approach to this challenge; the teacher 'should pose the question to the students and brainstorm ideas so we collaboratively reach solutions' (2003: 3). Ahlstrom continues to explain, 'place the themes on a list and ask the students to vote on which topic to cover next ... the students add more topics if they like, and they vote again' (Ahlstrom, 2003: 4). This seems like a good solution to the problem of time and relevance of the themes to discuss and learn about. Abby adds the following:

> I think we are working with a population that has dealt with many difficult things in their lives. Whether it's crossing the border illegally, leaving family behind, being told they can't go to school anymore because they're not smart enough, they can't learn, and they're now in a country they don't know. Their children are translating and speaking for them. So, they're fearful. A lot of them have not gone out without someone because they're scared of having to speak English. So, it's important when they come into my class that they know that they're safe to make mistakes.

Isserlis (2000) argues, 'regardless of an individual's experience with violence, torture, or abuse, being an adult learner is intimidating for many' (2000: 3). Adult ESL students should learn how to negotiate meaning and make sense of a conversation where they are listening to other people's life experiences to show empathy and to extrapolate new learning. In the ESL classroom, students can learn how to file a complaint, how to request a service and how to denounce injustice or violence. They should also learn about resources and organizations available to them that may assist in improving their individual life conditions. These are powerful reasons to get to know the students and to listen to their real-life learning needs. Abby reported the following during the interview:

> Ideally, we base our topics on student need; so, we identify their learning goal, and we ask why they are learning English. I'm trying to base my instruction more on that and growing in that area as a teacher. We are not required to use a specific textbook. I can do my planning with anything I want. That's why I'm able to draw on student interests and needs. And that's good and bad; it's a lot of work for me. I've been teaching for 13 years, and I still don't go and use my old lesson plans. I start like new every year! We have two sets of books for two different textbook series, and I have attempted to use these textbooks as my curriculum, but they are so grammar heavy! The procedures are basically the same ... Look at this picture. Listen to this dialogue. Answer these questions. Do this writing sample. Have this conversation. Next thing: Same! This method is not appropriate for the population of students we have at the learning center.

Even though Abby is an experienced teacher, not having a predetermined curriculum or a clear curricular plan to teach ESL adds more work to her job. It is important to negotiate the curriculum with the students to attend to their learning needs; however, when embarking in negotiation practices, teachers should not go empty handed (Harris, 2010). Negotiating the curriculum implies flexibility from the part of the instructors and a give and take between them and the learners. Therefore, in an ideal situation, there would be a pre-established curriculum to negotiate. Moreover, curriculum negotiation encompasses a discussion about teacher and students' roles and responsibilities, not just a discussion of the content to cover in a lesson.

In addition, recent emphasis on the implementation of content standards aims to ensure the quality of the content provided to adult learners (Center for Applied Linguistics, 2010: x). Content standards specify what learners should know and be able to do in certain subject or practical domains. Program standards specify the components of quality ESL programs. The most recently issued ESL Content Standards in Texas aim to describe what individuals can do with language in terms of listening, speaking, reading and writing for personal and career purposes (Texas Workforce Commission, 2016). This coming year (2018–2019) will be Abby's first year implementing content standards since her program funder will enforce it. The ideal situation would be that Abby uses the standards to organize her teaching around the language components that students need to master and still uses the themes and inquiries proposed by the learners. The standards should not get in the way of what and how to learn but inform the language competences that the learners need to achieve.

Conclusion

Abby's case study describes her work conditions and the challenges of teaching ESL in publicly funded adult education organizations. While describing her program, the education services and the students, she speaks about important issues such as negotiating the curriculum and working with female learners who are mothers and immigrants. As illustrated by the narratives provided through interviewing Abby, negotiation of the adult ESL curriculum requires close collaboration with students to ensure that the topics selected for teaching are meaningful to them. The ESL program and funder may specify the components of quality instruction, but the teacher should have the autonomy to negotiate with the students how to master these components. The teacher should be able to provide instruction that is relevant to the learner's life conditions as immigrants and adults. After all, curriculum negotiation is not a static process and what works for a group may not work for another.

Recommendations for Practice

(1) Create a safe learning environment based on respect and trust so that the ESL learners feel comfortable discussing and learning real-life topics.
(2) Including the learners' needs when planning instruction is considered a best teaching practice; however, it is important for the teacher to also have a curriculum to use for negotiation purposes.

(3) Become familiar with program expectations, funding policies and student expectations. Keeping all these in mind may be helpful in coming up with a curriculum that can benefit all who are involved in the teaching–learning process.
(4) Reflect on what curriculum negotiation means and how to implement it in your work setting.

Discussion Questions (Group Activity)

(1) Abby relied on her knowledge of communication processes when teaching ESL; besides your teaching skills, what other skill or knowledge can you bring and be confident incorporating when teaching language to adult learners?
(2) How do you use adult ESL content standards to plan instruction?
(3) How can ESL content standards help a teacher like Abby design an appropriate curriculum for the ESL course level they are teaching?
(4) According to your 'reading of the class dynamics', what are some generative themes that you could use to design lesson plans for a class you teach?

10 Conclusion

Learners' and Teachers' Voices

The case studies presented in this book were embedded in community-based programs and took place in a variety of settings, such as community centers, literacy and ESL programs, religious settings and libraries. These community education settings offer adults the opportunity to further their knowledge, become competent in their skills and examine cultural values and world concepts to create a better life, advancing them as individuals, as family members and community members. There are many reasons why adult immigrants need to learn English. These include: (a) to add a powerful tool to be able to use their talents while adapting to the host community; (b) to be able to compete for economic and educational opportunities; (c) to develop communication skills useful for their day-to-day interactions at work, school and social lives; (d) to realize their full potential as individuals and community members; and (e) to participate in democracy, obtain services and contribute to the economy of the country. ESL teachers should understand these learning needs and be adequately prepared to support and assist adult learners to achieve these goals. Thus, the main goal of this book was to document the experiences of adult English learners and teachers to share highlights from their learning and teaching journeys that are useful to graduate students and practitioners.

Part 1: Learners' Voices

In Part 1, learners' voices were presented through the narratives of actual ESL adult students. The teaching–learning approaches described in these chapters were learner-centered. Learners' Voices described strategies to help struggling readers like Alberto to view reading as an integral and fun part of an adult's daily routine. In Chapter 2, Alberto's case study illustrated his transformation in learning to enjoy reading. The instructor encouraged the reading activities that the students did outside of class because this was reading for pleasure and exposed the learners to different reading genres and reading activities. In Chapter 3, Doña Inés's story provided readers with knowledge on how to engage adult learners in active learning and participation. The chapter narrated the experiences of adult learners with emergent literacy skills and how the teacher used dialogic practices and storytelling to conduct the class. The teacher utilized reading comprehension strategies and reading topics familiar to the learners to build on their personal connection to these topics and promote class participation. Likewise, Chapter 4 highlighted intergenerational literacy as a practice for adult learners with low literacy skills to build confidence using English to communicate with others. This chapter presented different activities to focus on confidence building (e.g. speaking on the phone, learning new words, reading with relatives, creating a storybook and doing poster presentations). The author argued that the language classroom is the appropriate place to assist adult learners to develop confidence and practice strategies that can help them master the use of L2 in their daily activities outside of class. The last chapter in Part 1, Chapter 5, addressed learners' motivations and challenges attending adult education programs and learning ESL. This chapter reported adult ESL learners' motivations to center around family and economic progress, personal and professional promotion, and the relevance of the topics studied in the ESL class. In addition, the chapter revealed motivations unique to the learners' identities and individual stories as immigrants and L2 learners.

Part 2: Teachers' Voices

Part 2 of this book presented the narratives of directors, coordinators and teachers in different adult education programs. They spoke about challenges, such as a lack of space to offer adult education services, the need for continual professional development for the staff and teachers in their programs, the learners' participation in education opportunities or lack thereof, shortage of instructors, space and funding issues. These settings provided multiple adult education services such as ESL classes, citizenship and GED preparation, computer classes and resume writing, to mention a few. All of these programs promoted the development of literate communities and served as spaces for assisting teacher-learners in their journeys for professional socialization. Therefore, Part 2 also documented the experiences of novice TESOL teachers learning the profession and their journeys in learning how to become effective teachers. Therefore, in Chapter 6, Mary and Sarah described an ESL program housed in a Catholic church and a federally funded refugee program run by a religious organization. Their stories spoke to the challenges they faced, such as lack of instructors, lack of space, student attrition, the need for professional development and the need to provide extended educational services to newly arrived immigrants. Another relevant topic discussed in this chapter was the benefits for refugee adults and families when they participate in community garden activities. Chapter 7 presented challenges and successes offering adult education programs through a public library. Daisy discussed technology anxiety, the diverse needs of all library patrons and the learning needs of immigrants. An aspect worth highlighting from her narrative deals with difficulties when trying to implement the principles of self-directed learning with adults using technology to learn by themselves. In this case study, there was the need to assess the level of library patrons' self-directedness in becoming fully independent using technology to study for the GED. With adult education policies continually changing and budget cuts to adult education programs, libraries continue to play an important role in offering a variety of programs and literacy instruction to adults and families in the local communities. Chapter 8 described the experiences of teacher-learners practicing engaged scholarship to enhance their training as ESOL instructors of adult learners. The chapter documented novice teachers' experiences while they conducted classroom observations, served as tutors and conversation partners, and participated in internship practices. These narratives illustrated engaged scholarship as a door to collaboration, professional growth and reciprocal learning. Participating in real-life teaching situations and keeping a reflection journal proved to be important learning experiences to build confidence in becoming effective TESOL instructors. Finally, Chapter 9 discussed ESL curriculum negotiation within the context and constraints of federally funded adult education programs. Abby, an experienced ESL instructor, shared her journey becoming an English teacher. Her narratives illustrated the use of dialogue to come up with an emergent theme-based curriculum that focused on learner characteristics, program requirements and student learning needs. Thus, curriculum negotiation emerged as a student-centered practice in which teacher and students are both responsible for teaching and learning. Curriculum negotiation related to the what (content), the how (pedagogy), the who (learner-centered) and the why (relevant and/or required).

Emergent Themes Discussed in the Book Chapters

Within the context of community-based programs, all of the classes and programs where the narratives took place were offered free of charge, and their geographical locations influenced who attended them. As described in the different chapters, Central Texas welcomes a variety of adult immigrants. The programs and learners faced multiple challenges, but these were not the focus for telling their stories. The learners and teachers told about their efforts to succeed in learning and teaching ESL. They appeared to be resourceful and effective problem solvers. The central themes discussed in the different chapters included learning to enjoy reading, supporting adults with low literacy skills, boosting adult learners' confidence, adult ESL learners' motivations, refugee community gardening, professional development and other needs, putting theory into practice and curriculum negotiation.

Learning to enjoy reading

Reading is a fundamental activity in the life of any adult. However, reading in a second language brings more challenges when the learners do not have a positive attitude towards reading. Therefore, ESL teachers need to know how to address this issue. They need to expose the learners to a variety or reading genres, a variety of reading activities and reading strategies to help them find a genre or reading activity that they can enjoy. The activities described in Chapter 2 emphasized the importance for learners of practicing reading inside and outside the classroom. In this case, the instructor provided strategies for the learners to keep a record of what they read. She helped them discover the usefulness of reading and how it could become both pleasurable and a hobby. Adult ESL learners need to read for a purpose; this will increase their motivation to read outside the classroom. The teacher needs to find out when the learners read and for what purposes to be able to explain to them how reading connects to their daily lives as adults. In addition, the teacher needs to include activities that require reading to be able to accomplish a task such as providing an oral report or bringing a reading from home to practice silent reading during class time.

Supporting adults with low literacy skills

Adults with low literacy skills tend to be timid and participate very sporadically in class. Their reading and writing skills need extra work, and they can benefit from utilizing a storytelling approach that motivates them to write down their lived experiences with the purpose of sharing them with an authentic audience (e.g. family members, classmates, people who care about them and would be willing to listen). As described in Chapter 3, these learners can benefit from a developmental approach to writing. They can start with simple activities such as keeping a journal where they can write short sentences, draw pictures and take note of phrases or new words that they want to learn. Then, they can continue with more challenging activities such as writing a recipe, writing a guided poem or writing a short letter. Once they are able to connect writing with a personal aspect of their lives, they will feel more encouraged to move from oral language to print. Achieving this goal will require scaffolding and planning on the part of the teacher. A temporary strategy would be pairing up the learner with a more advanced classmate to learn from each other. The teacher can also serve as the more advanced peer. The learners can audio-record their thoughts and try to transcribe these ideas. Dictation and copying from the blackboard are also good writing practices. However, teachers need to make sure that these are done for authentic purposes. For instance, dictation happens in real life when we listen to others providing directions or useful information, or when copying a recipe from the internet or a book of recipes that is not ours. No matter the activity, there must be a connection to activities that could potentially happen in real life.

Boosting adult learners' confidence

In Chapter 4, implementing family literacy and authentic classroom practices were crucial activities in helping the adults participating in the reading project to feel confident in their ability to use English to communicate in public. In their interaction with other adults, English learners may feel doubtful and inadequate trying to accomplish a task that requires the use of English in public. The classroom is the appropriate place to assist them to develop this confidence and practice strategies that can help them in their daily activities outside of class. Role playing and interacting with a partner or family member can be beneficial for these adults. Activities such as practicing speaking on the phone, reading aloud to children, a spouse or a relative, storytelling, and doing poster presentations in class are appropriate to boosting adult learners' confidence to speak English in public. When adult English learners' confidence improves, they feel encouraged to take the next step in participating in more ambitious learning goals; often, they continue to obtain a GED and attend computer and citizenship classes. They also start to feel more open to putting themselves in situations requiring them to use what they learned in class such as running errands, going shopping and interacting with people in their neighborhood and their jobs. Boosting adult learners' confidence could seem like a difficult goal to accomplish but, with the appropriate class activities, it is possible. However, maintaining constant dialogue with the learners to design classroom activities that they find relevant is crucial.

Adult ESL learners' motivations

In Chapter 5, all learners, regardless of their sex, exhibited a strong desire to learn L2. They put their best efforts into attending the ESL classes, and they had a very positive attitude towards learning English. They were optimistic that they could achieve their goals, and they believed that attending the classes would help them achieve their goals of learning L2 and more. They were motivated by the love for their families, the need to communicate with their children, and their ambition to do better at work and have a better future. They wanted to become better versions of themselves as L2 conversationalists. Becoming fluent in English would add to their confidence to do better at work and attain their ideal L2 selves in this area. The social and familial aspects of their motivation to learn were strong forces to improve their language performance as well. They all wanted to improve their living conditions in the host country. They felt the urgency to communicate in English in the communities where they lived; they wanted to use what they had learned immediately after class. They were motivated to learn ESL through desire, effort and positive attitudes. Instrumental and integrative motivations fueled their desire to learn the language. They wanted to learn English to communicate with community members and were moved by integrative motivation to create a sense of belonging and adaptation. Their immigration stories, their desire to achieve their ideal L2 selves and their unique journeys as immigrants propelled them to continue learning. The teachers also contributed to increasing their motivation by building strong relationships based on trust and respect and by applying a learner-centered approach to teaching L2. They made sure the classes were engaging and were attentive listeners to foster the students' learning motivation.

Refugee community gardening

Religious-based organizations serve a large number of immigrants, and refugees are among those they serve. In fact, in 2016, 85,000 refugees were accepted in the United States, and Texas was first among the top seven states resettling refugees (Pew Research Center, 2016). Texas received the largest number of refugees (1779) in 2016. Accordingly, Chapter 6 provides a description of issues affecting refugee programs and the strategies that work when teaching refugees who are also English learners. The creation of a community garden as a learning space allowed Sarah to address some difficulties she was facing trying to engage her students in language learning for authentic communication. The community garden became a space to share cultural traditions, support family literacy development, learn about local plants and grow vegetables, plants and herbs from other counties. It allowed the learners to exchange recipes and to share a meal together. Sarah became a linguistic, cultural and community bridge to connect her learners with each other and their new living environment. Creating a community garden is just one example of social activities that teachers can promote with a similar group of learners. The goal is to find ways to connect to students' interests and realities. Teachers can help adults to acquire language skills, integrate in the community and develop social and navigational capitals useful to them once the classes come to an end. Immigration entails different levels of trauma, cultural shock and adaptation to the host community that may be difficult to overcome by just studying language in the artificial environment provided by the classroom setting.

Professional development and other needs

The need for continual professional development for teachers, the lack of space to provide services and the challenges that come with funding emerged as pressing concerns for adult education programs offering ESL instruction. These three issues became evident in the narratives of the adult ESL teachers in the case studies presented in Chapters 6 and 7. In Chapter 6, Janet explained that only two of the instructors in her program had appropriate credentials to teach ESL. All eight teachers were unpaid volunteers, and as a result, they were not required to attend training. Also, in Chapter 6, Sarah explained that there was an assumption that the instructor would 'learn on the go' how to become an effective teacher in the refugee program where she worked. Furthermore, in Chapter 7, Daisy reported needing to know how to instruct GED and ESL learners to use technology, so they could become self-directed learners. In her case, the public library staff and teachers could benefit from receiving training to prepare the adult learners to use technology to learn without the constant presence of a teacher. In addition, these teachers and staff members needed to gain knowledge about how self-directed learning works and how to instruct the learners to be successful using this combination of resources, technology and self-directedness in learning. In summary, the professional development needs of teachers and staff working at community-based adult education programs are many. Knowing how to speak the language, having experience as teachers or holding a university degree is not enough. Professional development must be a continual practice helping teachers and staff to keep up to date in the new advances in language learning and teaching and relevant immigration policies, just to mention a few areas of need. As described in the different chapters, each of these teaching/learning settings is different, serves a wide range of individuals and requires a different set of skills and knowledge from the teacher. Therefore, professional development should be tailored to these many needs.

Putting theory into practice

Chapter 8 described a few learning activities that have proved useful when training TESOL teachers and that use a balanced theory–practice approach. The theory provided in the university classroom is important; however, theory must come to life through practice. To this effect, the teacher-learners participated in a variety of learning experiences such as keeping a reflection journal, conducting classroom observations, tutoring adult English learners, serving as conversation partners for ESL adults and participating in internships. These learning activities have the potential for becoming creative solutions to the lack of professional development for ESL teachers in different programs. In particular, the novice instructors had a chance to learn from more experienced teachers, to design authentic lessons and to interact with actual adult learners. They had the opportunity to practice and question the theory they were reading and learning at the university. In addition, regardless of their levels of expertise, all TESOL instructors can benefit from keeping a reflection journal, participating in peer observation, having dialogue with colleagues and substituting classes for their colleagues to learn about learners in other language levels and courses. The reflection journal could work as an individual private activity or could be shared with trusted colleagues. This is a personal activity and has the potential to assist the teachers to reflect, change and improve their teaching practices. Keeping a reflection journal is an essential practice that teachers should use throughout their careers.

Curriculum negotiation

In Chapter 9, Abby described educators' precarious work conditions in publicly funded adult education organizations. Often, they need to hold multiple jobs to be able to pay their bills. Another aspect worth highlighting from her narrative is the close relationship she builds with the learners and how this allows her to decide on the teaching topics and class activities. After class hours, Abby keeps in touch with the students through texting and voicemail. Her main goal is to teach relevant topics that reflect the life experiences and learning needs of the adult English learners in her class. Even though Abby is an experienced instructor, not having a predetermined curriculum to teach ESL adds another layer of complexity to her job. She reinvents the lessons year after year. Negotiating the curriculum to include her students' learning needs would work better if Abby had a predetermined curriculum. For example, ESL content standards may prove helpful for her to develop a flexible curriculum that satisfies the demands of the program funder and the learning needs and goals of her learners. Regardless of program and funding requirements, Abby will continue to offer quality ESL education for her students because she is inquisitive and reflective, enjoys teaching, is open to learning and genuinely cares about the adult English learners she serves.

Theoretical Connections

Engaged scholarship

Most of the research projects documented in this book followed the principles of engaged scholarship (Boyer, 1996; Elwell & Bean, 2001; Lebeau & Bennion, 2014; Udall *et al.*, 2015). In the practice of engaged scholarship, the university professor makes the conscious decision to look for opportunities to work with local communities and take the students out of the classroom to apply their learning in the real world where theory becomes relevant. For example, in Chapter 8, novice TESOL teachers engaged in reciprocal learning, exchanged resources and practiced teaching. They applied theoretical knowledge to real-world experiences in community-based adult education programs and used these experiences to inform theory (Elwell & Bean, 2001). The professor and graduate students had a chance to gain direct knowledge of what was happening in actuality in the different local adult education programs instead of just reading it in a book or journal article. The English learners benefited from the opportunity to have extra practice to learn the language. The teachers contributed to increasing their English learners' motivation by building strong relationships based on trust and respect and by applying a learner-centered approach to teaching ESL. The experienced teachers received help from a novice teacher by designing lessons together, learning about new resources and technology, and by reflecting on their teaching practices. One of the main goals of engaged scholarship is to combine resources to address a social issue and, in this case, to provide high-quality L2 teaching and literacy instruction to the adults attending the community-based adult education programs. The collaboration also entailed learning from and with each other. Thus, the projects promoted stronger relationships with local adult education and literacy organizations, and opened doors for learning, teaching, research and collaboration opportunities.

Freirean pedagogy

Dialogue is at the center of Freirean pedagogy; 'dialogue is where humans meet to reflect on their reality as they make and remake it' (Shor & Freire, 1987: 98). A dialogical approach to learning and teaching was relevant to most concepts presented in this book. Specifically, in Chapter 4, the intergenerational reading project illustrated the need for the participating adults to improve their public speaking skills to gain the needed confidence to express themselves in public. In collaboration with children, these adults created storybooks, presented their stories in public at the school's faculty meeting and did poster presentations in class. They felt pride in sharing their personal experiences and immigration stories with others. Through using a variety of reading strategies and dialogic practices, parents and children were able to grow closer as a family. These adults acquired strategies to read, speak and present ideas in public. In Chapter 6, Sarah utilized the learners' prior knowledge and talents through creating the community garden and transformed this space as a focus for teaching and learning in dialogue. This teacher and the refugee ESL learners realized that learning in the classroom was too artificial and disconnected from their prior experiences coming from an agrarian tradition. The teaching strategies described in Chapters 4, 6 and 9 illustrate the teachers' capacity for developing strategies for transformation and dialogic practices. Exchanging ideas and socializing were triggers to using L2 to communicate for authentic purposes. For example, in Chapter 9, Abby negotiates the ESL curriculum with the learners in her class by listening and taking note of the learning needs and inquiries manifested by her students. Through an emerging theme-based curriculum, she develops trusting relationships for effective curriculum negotiation founded on two-way dialogue. All of the case studies presented in the book put the learners at the center of the teaching situation. All of the teachers and staff were eager to participate in dialogue to learn from each other. Humbly, they recognized that they needed further training, and that they needed to continue learning to do a good job providing for the needs of ESL adults and their families.

Second language acquisition theory

Second language acquisition theory guided the creation of all of the narratives presented in this book. More specifically, communicative language teaching practices were emphasized. The narratives strived to present a balance of activities and stories illustrating efforts to teach form and function but favored using L2 to communicate for authentic purposes. For example, in Chapter 5, it became evident that the adult immigrant learners had a positive attitude about work and life and were eager to learn English. They all wanted to improve their living conditions and made it a goal to enjoy both attending the ESL class and doing homework that was applicable to their specific life conditions. The teachers emphasized communication over grammar teaching and were aware of the many factors influencing SLA such as learner characteristics, sociocultural environment, L1 and L2 structures, opportunities to practice L2 with native speakers or more advanced peers, and constructive feedback (Lightbown & Spada, 2013). They focused on helping the learners understand cultural nuances, avoiding communication breakdown and applying grammar in an authentic context (Moss & Ross-Feldman, 2003). For instance, in Chapter 9, Abby made sure to center class activities on language acquisition practices. Communication was paramount in her class and an important aspect of creating a safe learning environment. Abby tried to keep the feelings of anxiety and fear of speaking in English as low as possible. This created a space for the learners to talk about topics such as their immigration stories, acculturation struggles, family issues and personal trauma. A communicative approach to teaching a language invites the learners to use their personal experiences in language learning (Nunan, 1991). As it became evident in the different book chapters, language learning was meaningful because the participating adults were able to make connections to their real lives, goals and learning needs.

Future Research

A closer look at the emergent themes discussed in the different chapters made it possible to identify themes deserving further consideration. These include benefits of setting goals in ESL learning, reading for pleasure and ESL learning, adult English learners building confidence, the impact of technology in GED and adult ESL learning, and the reflection journal as a tool for professional development.

Chapter 2 briefly discussed the importance of encouraging adult English learners to set learning goals from day one. However, a larger study focusing on the positive effects that result from learning to develop and follow through ESL learning goals would be beneficial.

A qualitative study documenting the benefits and uses of reading for pleasure to learn ESL was not available. Such a study documenting the systematic implementation and benefits of this practice would be helpful for TESOL practitioners and other experts working in adult learning settings.

A study focusing on helping adult English learners build confidence to use English in public is another idea for future research. The case study presented in Chapter 4 was framed within family literacy practices. A study examining how to foster confidence in public speaking within the context of publicly funded adult education programs is overdue. Adults need to use English in many public scenarios and TESOL teachers can benefit from these findings.

Another idea for future research is to examine the impact of using technology in GED and adult ESL learning. How can teachers train ESL learners to feel confident to use technology for GED practice and ESL learning without the constant presence of a teacher? How can teachers utilize self-directed learning principles to prepare learners to be independent and goal oriented to use technology as a tool for GED and ESL learning?

Finally, research on how to use the reflection journal as a tool for professional development would be worth documenting. Findings from such a study would be beneficial for TESOL practitioners and for those who do not have access to professional development opportunities. This could become a practice for colleagues to reflect and learn together.

Concluding Thoughts

This book illustrates how theory and practice merge and are interdependent. Focusing on language pedagogy and utilizing a humanistic approach to learning and teaching, the participants in the different case studies described the challenges and successes of adult English learners and teachers so that the readers can learn and transfer the lessons they consider appropriate. Depicting learners' voices and teachers' voices aimed to inform both points of view. The goal is to emphasize the importance of teachers being open to learning from their students and to reflect on how to improve their teaching practices every term.

Putting this work forward, I hope to encourage dialogue and discussion about important issues affecting learners, practitioners and researchers in the field of adult ESL. I am positive that each of us can make change possible. We can offer quality ESL education to adults in the United States even under the constraints of time, space, resources, policy and politics. As Freire (2004: 31) wrote: 'It is not possible to even think about transforming the world without a dream, without utopia, or without a vision'. All the people I know in this profession are putting forth their best effort to make this vision possible!

Appendix

Definition of Relevant Terms

It is important to provide clarification and facilitate understanding of relevant terms used throughout the book. This is not by any means an exhaustive list of terms associated with TESOL instruction and learning. Below, in alphabetical order, I present brief definitions of acronyms and relevant concepts.

EFL

EFL stands for 'English as a Foreign Language'. It is the use or study of the English language by non-native English speakers in countries in which English is not a local medium of communication (Richards & Rodgers, 2001).

ELL

This acronym means 'English Language Learner' and refers to students for whom English is not the native language and are faced with the specific task of learning English (Freeman *et al.*, 2002).

ESL

This stands for 'English as a Second Language'. This is the use or study of the English language by non-native speakers in countries such as the United States where English is the local language. Also, in this situation, the student is learning one more language after their native language (Richards & Rodgers, 2001).

ESOL

This term refers to English for Speakers of Other Languages (Crandall *et al.*, 2008). Many times, English is a third or fourth language for adult English learners.

Professional socialization

This refers to the process of becoming a professional. Brody *et al.* (2010) explain that professional socialization is 'the process of developing a role-based identity with values, norms, and symbols that may span many organizations within or across multiple fields. This type of socialization facilitates acquisition of the skills, knowledge, and attitudes necessary to fulfill the duties of this role' (2010: 615–616).

SLA

This acronym refers to 'second language acquisition' and the process by which people acquire a second language. It refers to learning any language in addition to a person's native language (Ellis & Fellow, 2008).

TESOL

This acronym stands for 'Teaching of English to speakers of other languages'. It is used to identify the educational training of teachers who wish to become instructors of English for learners who speak different languages, either native or non-native (Richards & Rodgers, 2001).

References

Abdullah, S., Rahim, P.R., Setia, R., Mohamad, R., Ghazali, N., Sabapathy, E., Nair, G.K., Muniandry, M.K., Theethappan, R., Wan Hassan, W.A. and Che Hassan, N.S. (2012) Reading for pleasure as a means of improving reading comprehension skills. *Canadian Center of Science and Education* 8 (13), 233–238.

Ahlstrom, C. (2003) Collaborating with students to build curriculum that incorporates real-life materials. *Focus on Basics* 6 (C), 1–7.

Akhtar, S. (2011) *Immigration and Acculturation: Mourning, Adaptation, and the Next Generation*. New York: Jason Aronson.

American Library Association. (2010) *Strategic Plan 2011–2015* (2009–2010 ALA CD#36.2). See http://www.ala.org/aboutala/sites/ala.org.aboutala/files/content/governance/policymanual/updatedpolicymanual/ocrpdfofprm/cd_36%202_2015_strateg.pdf

American Psychological Association, Presidential Task Force on Immigration (2012) *Crossroads: The Psychology of Immigration in the New Century*. See http://www.apa.org/topics/immigration/report/aspx

Armstrong, E. (2015) ESL and low-income computer literacy learners: A microcosm for adult learning in libraries? *Public Services Quarterly* 11 (2), 135–143. DOI: 10.1080/15228959.2015.1039748

Barkhuizen, G. (2007) A narrative approach to exploring context in language teaching. *ELT Journal* 62 (3), 231–239.

Barkhuizen, G. (2011) Narrative knowledging in TESOL. *Tesol Quarterly* 45 (3), 391–414.

Barkhuizen, G. (2014) Narrative research in language teaching and learning. *Language Teaching* 47 (4), 450–466.

Bax, S. (2003) The end of CLT: A context approach to language teaching. *ELT Journal* 57 (3), 278–287. DOI: 10.1093/elt/57.3.278

Bello, T. (2000) The importance of helping adult ESL students set goals (ERIC Document Reproduction Service no. ED445562).

Boomer, G., Lester, N., Onore, C. and Cook, J. (1992) *Negotiating the Curriculum: Educating for the 21st Century*. London: The Falmer Press.

Borg, S. (2001) The research journal: A tool for promoting and understanding researcher development. *Language Teaching Research* 5 (2), 156–177.

Boyer, E. (1990) *Scholarship Reconsidered: Priorities of the Professoriate*. Princeton, NJ: Carnegie Foundation for the Advancement of Teaching.

Boyer, E. (1996) The scholarship of engagement. *Journal of Public Service and Outreach* 1 (1), 11–20.

Breen, M.P. and Littlejohn, A. (2000) *Classroom Decision-making: Negotiation and Process Syllabuses in Practice*. Cambridge: Cambridge University Press.

Brody, J., Vissa, J. and Weathers, J. (2010) School leader professional socialization: The contribution of focused observations. *Journal of Research on Leadership Education* 5 (14), 611–651.

Brookfield, S.D. (2013) *Powerful Techniques for Teaching Adults*. San Francisco, CA: Jossey-Bass.

Brown, H.D. (2000) *Principles of Language Learning and Teaching* (4th edn). White Plains, NY: Addison Wesley Longman.

Brown, M.C. and Bywater, K. (2009/2010) Professionalism prevails in adult education ESL classrooms. *The CATESOL Journal* 21 (1), 202–211.

Burt, M., Peyton, J.K. and Schaetzel, K. (2008) *Working with Adult English Language Learners with Limited Literacy: Research, Practice, and Professional Development*. Washington, DC: Center for Applied Linguistics. See http://www.cal.org/caelanetwork/pdfs/LimitedLiteracyFinalWeb.pdf

Buttaro, L. and King, K.P. (2001) Understanding adult ESL learners: Multiple dimensions of learning and adjustments among Hispanic women. *Adult Basic Education* 11 (1), 40–60.

Carver, M.L. (2003) Not by curriculum alone. *Focus on Basics* 6 (C), 32–37.

Center for Applied Linguistics (2010) *Education for Adult English Language Learners in the United States: Trends, Research, and Promising Practices*. Washington, DC: Author.

Chao, X. and Kuntz, A. (2013) Church-based ESL programs as figured world: Immigrant adult learners, identity and power. *Linguistics and Education* 24 (4), 466–478. DOI: 10.1016/j.linged.2013.06.001

Chao, X. and Mantero, M. (2014) Church-based ESL adult programs: Social mediators for empowering 'family literacy ecology communities'. *Journal of Literacy Research* 46 (1), 90–114. DOI: 10.1177/1086296X14524588

Chapman, J., McGilp, P., Cartwright, P., De Souza, M. and Toomey, R. (2006) Overcoming barriers that impede participation in lifelong learning. In J. Chapman, P. Cartwright and E.J. McGilp (eds) *Lifelong Learning, Participation and Equity* (pp. 151–174). Rotterdam: Springer.

Cisneros, S. (2003) *The House on Mango Street*. New York, NY: Alfred A. Knopf.

Clark, C.M. and Rossiter, M. (2008) Narrative learning in adulthood. *New Directions for Adult and Continuing Education* 119 (Spring), 61–70. DOI: 10.1002/ace.306

Coatney, S. (2006) The importance of background knowledge. *Teacher Librarian* 34 (1), 60.

Coelho, P. (2004) *El Manual del Guerrero de la Luz/Warrior of the Light: A Manual*. New York, NY: HarperCollins Publishers.

Cook, J. (1992) Negotiating the curriculum: Programing for learning. In G. Boomer, N. Lester, C. Onore and J. Cook (eds) *Negotiating the Curriculum: Educating for the 21st Century* (pp. 15–31). London: The Falmer Press.

Cooter, K.S. (2006) When Mama can't read: Counteracting intergenerational illiteracy. *The Reading Teacher* 59 (7), 698–702. DOI: 10.1598/RT.59.7.9

Crandall, J., Ingersoll, G. and Lopez, J. (2008) *Adult ESL Teacher Credentialing and Certification*. Washington, DC: Center for Applied Linguistics. See http://www.cal.org/caela/esl_resources/briefs/tchrcred.html

Creswell, J.W. (2007) *Qualitative Inquiry and Research Design: Choosing Among Five Approaches* (2nd edn). Thousand Oaks, CA: Sage.

Creswell, J.W. (2013) *Qualitative Inquiry and Research Design: Choosing Among Five Approaches* (3rd edn). Los Angeles, CA: Sage.

Cutspec, P.A. (2004) Influences of dialogic reading on the language development of toddlers. *Bridges* 2 (1), 1–12.

Dörnyei, Z. (2003) Attitudes, orientations, and motivations in language learning: Advances in theory, research, and applications. *Language Learning* 53 (1), 3–32.

Dörnyei, Z. (2005) *The Psychology of the Language Learner: Individual Differences in Second Language Acquisition*. Mahwah, NJ: Erlbaum.

Ellis, R. (2008) *Second Language Acquisition*. Oxford: Oxford University Press.

Ellis, R. (2010) Second language acquisition, teacher education and language pedagogy. *Language Teaching* 43 (2), 182–201.

Ellis, R. and Fellow, F. (2008) *Principles of Instructed Second Language Acquisition*. Washington, DC: Center for Applied Linguistics. See http://www.cal.org/resources/digest/digest_pdfs/Instructed2ndLangFinalWeb.pdf

Elwell, D. and Bean, M.S. (2001) The efficacy of service-learning for community college ESL students. *Community College Review* 28 (4), 47–61.

Freeman, Y.S., Freeman, D.E. and Mercuri, S. (2002) *Closing the Achievement Gap: How to Reach Limited-formal-schooling and Long-term English Learners*. Portsmouth, NH: Heinemann.

Freire, P. (1970) *Pedagogy of the Oppressed*. New York: Continuum.

Freire, P. (1998) *Pedagogy of Freedom: Ethics, Democracy, and Civic Courage*. Lanham, MD: Rowman & Littlefield.

Freire, P. (2001) *Pedagogy of Freedom: Ethics, Democracy, and Civic Courage*. Lanham, MD: Rowman & Littlefield.

Friere, P. (2004) *Pedagogy of Indignation*. Boulder, CO: Paradigm.

Gadsen, V.L. (2000) Intergenerational literacy within families. In M.L. Kamil, P.B. Mosenthal, P.D. Pearson and R. Barr (eds) *Handbook of Reading Research* (Vol. 3, pp. 871–887). Mahwah, NJ: Erlbaum.

Galbraith, M.W. (1990) The nature of community and adult education. In M.W. Galbraith (ed.) *Education through Community Organizations* (pp. 3–11). San Francisco, CA: Jossey-Bass.

Gall, M.D., Gall, J.P. and Borg, W.R. (2010) *Applying Educational Research: How to Read, Do, and Use Research to Solve Problems of Practice* (6th edn). Boston, MA: Pearson.

Gardner, R.C. (1985) *Social Psychology and Language Learning: The Role of Attitudes and Motivation*. London: Edward Arnold.

Gardner, R.C. and Lambert, W. (1972) *Attitudes and Motivation in Second Language Learning*. Rowley, MA: Newbury House.

González, N., Moll, L.C. and Amanti C. (eds) (2005) *Funds of Knowledge: Theorizing Practices in Households, Communities, and Classrooms*. Mahwah, NJ: Erlbaum.

Gregg, K.R. (1984) Krashen's monitor and Occam's razor. *Applied Linguistics* 5, 79–100.

Grow, G.O. (1991) Teaching learners to be self-directed. *Adult Education Quarterly* 41 (3), 125–149.

Harris, H. (2010) Curriculum negotiation at NHK: Meeting the needs and demands of adult learners. *The Language Teacher* 34 (6), 22–26.

Hartwig, K.A. and Mason, M. (2016) Community gardens for refugee and immigrant communities as a means of health promotion. *Journal of Community Health* 41 (6), 1153–1159.

Isserlis, J. (2000) Trauma and the adult English language learner (report no. ED444397). Washington, DC: Center for Applied Linguistics. See ERIC database.

Jimenez, T.C., Filippini, A.L. and Gerber, M.M. (2006) Shared reading within Latino families: An analysis of reading interactions and language use. *Bilingual Research Journal* 30 (2), 431–452.

Kerka, S. (2000) *Incidental Learning. Trends And Issues Alert No. 18*. Washington, DC: Office of Educational Research and Improvement. See ERIC database (ED446234).

Krashen, S.D. (1985) *Principles and Practice in Second Language Acquisition*. Oxford: Pergamon Press.

Krashen, S.D. (1988) Do we learn to read by reading? The relationship between free reading and reading ability. In D. Tannen (ed.) *Linguistics in Context: Connecting Observation and Understanding* (pp. 269–298). Norwood, NJ: Ablex.

Krashen, S.D. (2003) *Explorations in Language Acquisition and Use*. Portsmouth, NH: Heinemann.

Krashen, S.D. (2009) *Principles and Practice in Second Language Acquisition*. Oxford: Pergamon Press. Downloaded from http://www.sdkrashen.com/content/books/principles_and_practice.pdf

Larrotta, C. (2007) Inquiry in the adult classroom: An ESL literacy experience. *Adult Learning* 17 (3/4), 25–29.

Larrotta, C. (2011) Second language vocabulary learning and teaching: Still a hot topic. *Journal of Adult Education, Information Series* 1 (40), 1–11.

Larrotta, C. and Serrano, A.F. (2011) Adult learners' funds of knowledge: The case of an English class for parents. *Journal of Adolescent and Adult Literacy* 55 (4), 316–325.

Larrotta, C., Moon, J.Y. and Huang, J. (2016) Learning a new language is like Swiss cheese: Learning to learn English. *Adult Learning* 27 (4), 168–174. DOI: 10.1177/1045159516643946

Larsen-Freeman, D. and Anderson, M. (2011) *Techniques & Principles in Language Teaching* (3rd edn). New York, NY: Oxford University Press.

Lebeau, Y. and Bennion, A. (2014) Forms of embeddedness and discourses of engagement: A case study of universities in their local environment. *Studies in Higher Education* 39 (2), 278–293.

Lightbown, P.M. and Spada, N. (2013) *How Languages are Learned* (4th edn). Oxford: Oxford University Press.

Lomas Garza, C. (1996) *In my Family/En mi Familia*. San Francisco, CA: Children's Book Press.

Liu, D. (2015) A critical review of Krashen's input hypothesis: Three major arguments. *Journal of Education and Human Development* 4 (4), 139–146.

Mackeracher, D. (2004) *Making Sense of Adult Learning* (2nd edn). Toronto: University of Toronto Press.

Mason, B. (2006) Free voluntary reading and autonomy in second language acquisition: Improving TOEFL scores from reading alone. *International Journal of Foreign Language Teaching* 2 (1), 2–5.

Mason, B. (2017) The effect of pleasure reading experience 30 years ago. *Turkish Online Journal of English Language Teaching (TOJELT)* 2 (3), 130–132.

McLaughlin, B. (1987) *Theories of Second-language Learning*. London: Edward Arnold.

Merriam, S.B. (2009) *Qualitative Research: A Guide to Design and Implementation*. San Francisco, CA: Jossey Bass.

Merriam, S.B., Caffarella, R.S. and Baumgartner, L.M. (2007) *Learning in Adulthood* (3rd edn). San Francisco, CA: Jossey-Bass.

Mezirow, J. and Associates (1990) *Fostering Critical Reflections in Adulthood: A Guide to Transformative and Emancipatory Learning*. San Francisco, CA: Jossey-Bass.

Milana, M. and McBain, L. (2014) Adult education in the United States of America: A critical examination of national policy (1998–2014). *Encyclopaideia* 18 (40), 34–52.

Moss, D. and Ross-Feldman, L. (2003) *Second Language Acquisition in Adults: From Research to Practice*. Washington, DC: Center for Applied Linguistics (ERIC Document Reproduction Service no. ED99-CO-0008).

Nayir, F. (2017) The relationship between student motivation and class engagement levels. *Eurasian Journal of Educational Research* 71, 59–77.

Neville, P., O'Dwyer, M. and Power, M.J. (2014) The social value of community-based adult education in Limerick City. *Adult Learner The Irish Journal of Adult and Community Education* 42–56.

Nguyen, N.T. (2011) Syllabus negotiation: A case study in a tertiary EFL context in Vietnam. *Education in Asia* 2 (1), 71–91.

Norman, A.C. (2012) Librarians' leadership for lifelong learning. *Public Library Quarterly* 31 (2), 91–140. DOI: 10.1080/01616846.2012.684577

Norton, B. (2000) *Identity and Language Learning: Gender, Ethnicity and Educational Change*. Harlow: Pearson Education.
Norton, B. (2013) *Identity and Language Learning: Extending the Conversation* (2nd edn). Bristol: Multilingual Matters.
Nunan, D. (1991) Communicative tasks and the language curriculum. *TESOL Quarterly* 25 (2), 279–295. DOI: 10.2307/3587464
Nunan, D. (2015) *Teaching English to Speakers of Other Languages: An Introduction*. New York, NY: Routledge.
O'Meara, K.A. and Rice, E. (2005) *Faculty Priorities Reconsidered: Rewarding Multiple Forms of Scholarship*. San Francisco, CA: Jossey-Bass.
Orem, R.A. (2005) *Teaching Adult English Language Learners*. Malabar, FL: Krieger.
Orman, S. (1998) *The 9 Steps to Financial Freedom*. New York, NY: Three Rivers Press.
Oughton, H. (2010) Funds of knowledge – A conceptual critique. *Studies in the Education of Adults* 42 (1), 63–78.
Packard, B.W. (2001) When your mother asks for another book: Fostering intergenerational exchange of culturally relevant books. *Journal of Adolescent & Adult Literacy* 44 (7), 626–633.
Patomella, A., Kottorp, A. and Nygård, L. (2013) Design and management features of everyday technology that challenge older adults. *British Journal of Occupational Therapy* 76 (9), 390–398. DOI: 10.4276/030802213X13782044946229
Patton, M.Q. (2002) *Qualitative Research & Evaluation Methods* (3rd edn). Thousand Oaks, CA: Sage.
Patton, M.Q. (2015) *Qualitative Research & Evaluation Methods: Integrating Theory and Practice* (4th edn). Thousand Oaks, CA: Sage.
Peich, A. and Fletcher, C.N. (2015) Public libraries and cooperative extension as community partners for lifelong learning and learning cities. *New Directions for Adult and Continuing Education* 145, 45–55. DOI: 10.1002/ace.20122
Peregoy, S.F. and Boyle, O.F. (2005) *Reading, Writing, and Learning in ESL: A Resource Book for K-12 Teachers* (4th edn). Upper Saddle River, NJ: Pearson Education.
Pew Research Center (2016) U.S. admits record number of Muslim refugees in 2016. See http://www.pewresearch.org/fact-tank/2016/10/05/u-s-admits-record-number-of-muslim-refugees-in-2016/
Poe, E.A. (1843) *The Tell-Tale Heart*. Boston, MA: Pioneer. Downloaded from https://www.eapoe.org/works/tales/thearta.htm
Richards, J.C. and Rodgers, T.S. (2001) *Approaches and Methods in Language Teaching* (2nd edn). New York, NY: Cambridge University Press.
Riessman, C.K. (2008) *Narrative Methods for the Human Sciences*. Los Angeles, CA: Sage.
Rossiter, M. (2002) *Narrative and Stories in Adult Teaching and Learning*. Columbus, OH: The Educational Resources Information Center. See ERIC database (ED473147).
Rossman, G.B. and Rallis, S.F. (2003) *Learning in the Field: An Introduction to Qualitative Research*. (2nd edn). Thousand Oaks, CA: Sage.
Savignon, S.J. (1997) *Communicative Competence: Theory and Classroom Practice*. New York, NY: McGraw-Hill.
Shor, I. and Freire, P. (1987) *A Pedagogy for Liberation: Dialogues on Transforming Education*. New York, NY: Bergin & Garvey.
Short, K.G., Harste, J.C. and Burke C. (1996) *Creating Classrooms for Authors and Inquirers*. Portsmouth, NH: Heinemann.
Shrestha, S. and Krolak, L. (2015) The potential of community libraries in supporting literate environments and sustaining literacy skills. *International Review of Education* 61 (3), 399–418. DOI: 10.1007/s11159-014-9462-9

Singhal, M. (2005) *Teaching Reading to Adult Second Language Learners: Theoretical Foundations, Pedagogical Applications, and Current Issues*. Lowell, MA: The Reading Matrix.

Spada, N. and Lightbown, P.M. (2010) Second language acquisition. In N. Schmitt (ed.) *An Introduction to Applied Linguistics* (2nd edn, pp. 108–123). Abingdon: Routledge.

Stake, R.E. (1994) Case Studies. In N.K. Denzin and Y.S. Lincoln (eds) *Handbook of Qualitative Research* (3rd edn, pp. 236–247). Thousand Oaks, CA: Sage.

Stake, R.E. (2005) Qualitative case studies. In N.K. Denzin and Y.S. Lincoln (eds) *Handbook of Qualitative Research* (3rd edn, pp. 443–466). Thousand Oaks, CA: Sage.

Stanton, T., Giles, D. and Cruz, N. (1999) *Service-learning: A Movement's Pioneers Reflect on Its Origins, Practice, and Future*. San Francisco, CA: Jossey-Bass.

Taylor-Powell, E. and Renner, M. (2003) Analyzing qualitative data. *University of Wisconsin Program Development & Evaluation*, 1–10.

Texas Workforce Commission (2016) *Texas Adult Education and Literacy Standards*. Austin, TX: Author.

Tisdell, E., Taylor, E.W. and Sprow, K. (2010) Financial literacy education for adult learners in community-based programs. National Endowment for Financial Education. See http://www.nefe.org/LinkClick.aspx?fileticket=CpQ83--pkBA%3D&tabid=1040

Tummala-Narra, P. (2014) Cultural identity in the context of trauma and immigration from a psychoanalytic perspective. *Psychoanalytic Psychology* 31 (3), 396–409.

Udall, J., Forrest, D. and Stewart, K. (2015) Locating and building knowledges outside of the academy: Approaches to engaged teaching at the University of Sheffield. *Teaching in Higher Education* 20 (2), 158–170.

United States Census Bureau (2014) *National Population Projection*. See https://www.census.gov/population/projections/data/national/2014.html

Ushioda, E. (2014) Motivational perspectives on the self in SLA: A developmental view. In S. Mercer and M. Williams (eds) *Multiple Perspectives on the Self in SLA* (pp. 127–141). Bristol: Multilingual Matters.

Vélez-Ibáñez, C.G. and Greenberg, J.B. (1992) Formation and transformation of funds of knowledge among U.S. Mexican households. *Anthropology & Education Quarterly* 23 (4), 313–335. DOI: 10.1525/aeq.1992.23.4.05x1582v

Wajnryb, R. (2003) *Stories: Narrative Activities for the Language Classroom*. Cambridge: Cambridge University Press.

White, L. (1987) Against comprehensible input: The input hypothesis and the development of second language competence. *Applied Linguistics* 8, 95–110.

Whitmore, K.F. and Crowell, C.G. (1994) *Inventing a Classroom: Life in a Bilingual Whole Language Learning Community*. York, ME: Stenhouse.

Worth, S.E. (2008) Storytelling and narrative knowing: An examination of the epistemic benefits of well-told stories. *Journal of Aesthetic Education* 42 (3), 42–56.

Yin, R.K. (2009) *Case Study Research: Design and Method* (4th edn). Thousand Oaks, CA: Sage.

Zanoni, J.P. (2007) Antonio Gramsci and funds of knowledge: Organic ethnographers of knowledge in workers' centres. Paper presented at the Third International Gramsci Society Conference, Sardinia, Italy.

Zevenbergen, A.A. and Whitehurst, G.J. (2003) Dialogic reading: A shared picture book reading intervention for pre-schoolers. In A. van Kleeck, S.A. Stahl and E.B. Bauer (eds) *On Reading Books to Children: Parents and Teachers*. Hillsdale, NJ: Lawrence Erlbaum.

Index

Note: Page numbers in *italics* indicate Figures and Tables.

Abdullah, S. 19, 20
acculturation support 70–71
acquisition-learning distinction
    hypothesis 6
adult education 77, 78–79, 80
affective filter hypothesis 7
Ahlstrom, C. 98, 99, 101, 106, 107–108
Akhtar, S. 105
American Library Association 76
American Psychological Association 105
Anderson, M. 6
Armstrong, E. 82, 83
assessments 22–23
attrition 67–68, 69, 102–104
autobiographical poems 30–31
autocorrection 6–7

background knowledge 27
Barkhuizen, G. 10–12
Bax, S. 6
Bean, M.S. 4, 86, 87, 88, 93, 118
Bello, T. 16
Bennion, A. 4, 86, 118
Boomer, G. 98
Borg, S. 85
Boyer, E. 4, 86, 87, 118
Breen, M.P. 99, 107
Brody, J. 85, 123
Brookfield, S.D. 83
Brown, H.D. 6
Brown, M.C. 68, 70, 100, 101
Burt, M. 32
Buttaro, L. 104, 105, 107
Bywater, K. 68, 70, 100, 101

Carver, M.L. 102, 106
case study method 7–8
Center for Applied Linguistics 101,
    102–103, 109
Chao, X. 65, 74

Chapman, J. 79
Clark, C.M. 26, 29
classroom observations 87–90, *88*
Coatney, S. 27, 29
communicative competence 6
communicative language teaching 6
community garden 71, 72–73, *72*, 116
community-based programs 15–16,
    76, 111
    see also engaged scholarship
conceptual framework 3–7
confidence
    community-based programs 15, 16
    family reading project 37–43, 115
    literacy class 29, 30
continuous learning 71, 96
    see also professional development
conversation club case study 48–53
conversation partners 92–94
Cook, J. 98
Cooter, K.S. 35
Crandall, J. 122
Creswell, J.W. 8, 9, 10
critical reflection 5, 87, 88–89
Crowell, C.G. 98
cultural adjustment 105
culture 18, 28–30
    see also acculturation support
curriculum negotiation 98–99, 100–101,
    102, 106–109, 118
Cutspec, P.A. 35

data analysis process 9–10
data collection sources 8
deductive analysis 10
dialogue 5, 26, 119
dictation 39
discrimination 105
disorienting dilemma 105
Dörnyei, Z. 46–47

EFL, definition 122
ELL, definition 122
Ellis, R. 6, 7, 45, 46, 123
Elwell, D. 4, 86, 87, 88, 93, 118
emergent theme-based curriculum 101
engaged scholarship 4, 86–96, 118–119
enrollment 102–104
ESL, definition 122
ESOL, definition 122–123
evening class case study 53–59

family reading project 36–44, 115, 119
   phone conversations 38
   poster presentations 41–42
   reading with children 39–40
   storybooks 40–41
   vocabulary development 38–39
Fellow, F. 7, 123
Fletcher, C.N. 76, 79
Freeman, Y.S. 122
Freire, P. 26, 69, 86, 87, 89, 91–92, 106, 119, 121
Freirean pedagogy 4–5, 119–120
funding 77, 78, 80–81
funds of knowledge 20–21, 26
future research 120–121

Gadsen, V.L. 35
Galbraith, M.W. 15
Gall, M.D. 7
gardening program 71, 72–73, 72, 116
Gardner, R.C. 45, 46
gender *see* immigrant women
generative themes 106
González, N. 20
grammar 6, 98–99
Greenberg, J.B. 20
Grow, G.O. 83

Harris, H. 98, 99, 106, 107, 108
Hartwig, K.A. 71, 73

identity 47–48
immigrant women 105–107
immigrants 74
   learning needs 82, 83
   reasons to learn English 111
     (*see also* motivation)
incidental learning 22
inductive analysis 10
input hypothesis 7

inquiry cycles project 21–22
instrumental case study 8
instrumental motivation 46, 48–50, 53–55, 58–59
integrative motivation 46, 50–53, 55–56, 59
intergenerational reading 35, 119
   see also family reading project
internship practices 94–96
intrinsic motivation 46
Isserlis, J. 105, 106, 108

Jimenez, T.C. 35

Kerka, S. 22
King, K.P. 104, 105, 107
Kingdom of the Golden Dragon, The (Allende) 18–19
knowledge
   background knowledge 27
   funds of knowledge 20–21, 26
Krashen, S.D. 6–7, 19, 20
Krolak, L. 76

Lambert, W. 45
language acquisition 6
language as interactive tool 1
language learning process 6–7
language teaching 1, 6
Larrotta, C. 20, 21, 22, 39, 100
Larsen-Freeman, D. 6
learners
   attrition 67–68, 69, 102–104
   demographics 104–105
   identity 47–48
   relationship with teachers 26–29, 54–55, 56–58, 93–94, 104, 106
   retention 17
learning 6
   incidental 22
   lifelong 79
   self-directed 83
learning goals 16–17
learning needs 82–83
Lebeau, Y. 4, 86, 118
libraries 76–84, 117
   funding 77, 78, 80–81
   patrons' learning needs 82–83
lifelong learning 79
Lightbown, P.M. 6, 120
listening 5

literacy *see* reading; writing
literacy class 25, 114–115
   learners' knowledge 26–29
   teaching strategies 32–33
   writing 29–31
Littlejohn, A. 99, 107
Liu, D. 7

Mackeracher, D. 20, 45
Mantero, M. 65, 74
Mason, B. 19, 20
Mason, M. 71, 73
McBain, L. 101
megacommunities 15
Merriam, S.B. 7, 8, 9, 15
Mexican coin *18*
Mezirow, J. 105
Milana, M. 101
monitor hypothesis 6–7
Mondopads 80–82, *81*, 83
Moss, D. 5–6, 16, 120
motivation 17, 21, 45–48, 115–116

narrative 8–12
   see also oral language; storytelling
narrative knowledging 11
National Population Projection report 74
natural order hypothesis 6
Nayir, F. 45
Neville, P. 15
Nguyen, N.T. 99, 106, 107
Norman, A.C. 76
Norton, B. 47
Nunan, D. 6, 98, 99, 104, 120

O'Meara, K.A. 4
oral language
   conversation club case study 48–53
   conversation partners 92–94
   literacy class 28
   see also narrative; storytelling
Orem, R.A. 68, 90
Oughton, H. 26

Packard, B.W. 35
participation 102–104
Patomella, A. 82
Patton, M.Q. 8, 10
Peich, A. 76, 79
Pew Research Centre 73, 116
phone conversations 38

poems 30–31
poster presentations 41–42
Presidential Task Force on Immigration 105
professional development 68–69, 116–117
professional socialization 85
professionalism 68
public engagement *see* engaged scholarship
public libraries 76–84, 117
   funding 77, 78, 80–81
   patrons' learning needs 82–83

Rallis, S.F. 8
reading 114
   for pleasure 17–21
   role of background knowledge in 27
   as a tool 21–22
   see also intergenerational reading
reading project 36–44, 115, 119
   poster presentations 41–42
   reading with children 39–40
   storybooks 40–41
   vocabulary development 38–39
reading strategies 28–29
recipes 29–30
recreational reading *see* reading: for pleasure
reflection *see* critical reflection
refugee arrivals, USA 73–74, 73, 116
refugee program 69–74, 116
religious organizations 65–74
   refugee program 69–74, 116
Renner, M. 9
retention 17
Rice, E. 4
Richards, J.C. 122, 123
Riessman, C.K. 9
Rodgers, T.S. 122, 123
Ross-Feldman, L. 5–6, 16, 120
Rossiter, M. 26, 29
Rossman, G.B. 8

Savignon, S.J. 6
scholarship *see* engaged scholarship
second language acquisition (SLA) 5–7, 120, 123
self-correction 6–7
self-directed learning 83
Serrano, A.F. 20, 21
Shor, I. 119

Short, K.G. 21
Shrestha, S. 76
Singhal, M. 27
SMART goals 15–16
songs 39
Spada, N. 6, 120
speaking *see* narrative; oral language; storytelling
Stake, R.E. 7, 8
Stanton, T. 88
storybooks 40–41
storytelling 26, 28–29, 30–31
  see also narrative; oral language

task motivation 46–47
Taylor-Powell, E. 9
teachers
  confidence 69, 91–92, 94
  continuous learning 71, 96
  income 80
  professional background 101
  professional development 68–69, 116–117
  professionalism 68
  relationship with learners 26–29, 54–55, 56–58, 93–94, 104, 106
  work conditions 99–100
teaching materials 32
technology 80–82, *81*, 82–83, 117
TESOL, definition 123
TESOL instructor training 85–96, 117–118, 118–119
  classroom observations 87–90, *88*
  conversation partners 92–94

internship practices 94–96
tutoring sessions 90–92
tests 22–23
Texas Workforce Commission (TWC) 78–79, 102, 109
Tisdell, E. 15
trauma 105, 106
Tummala-Narra, P. 105
tutoring sessions 90–92

Udall, J. 4, 86, 87, 89, 94, 96
university faculty *see* engaged scholarship; family reading project
Ushioda, E. 45

Vélez-Ibáñez, C.G. 20
vocabulary development 38–39
voluntary reading *see* reading: for pleasure

Wajnryb, R. 9
Whitehurst, G.J. 35
Whitmore, K.F. 98
women 105–107
Worldwide Refugee Admissions Processing System 74
Worth, S.E. 8
writing 29–31, 114

Yin, R.K. 8

Zanoni, J.P. 20
Zevenbergen, A.A. 35

For Product Safety Concerns and Information please contact our EU Authorised Representative:

Easy Access System Europe

Mustamäe tee 50

10621 Tallinn

Estonia

gpsr.requests@easproject.com